Engaging 'Hard to Reach' Parents

Engaging 'Hard to Reach' Parents

Teacher–Parent Collaboration to Promote Children's Learning

Anthony Feiler

A John Wiley & Sons, Ltd., Publication

This edition first published 2010
© 2010 John Wiley & Sons Ltd

Wiley-Blackwell is an imprint of John Wiley & Sons, formed by the merger of Wiley's global Scientific, Technical, and Medical business with Blackwell Publishing.

Registered Office
John Wiley & Sons Ltd, The Atrium, Southern Gate, Chichester, West Sussex, PO19 8SQ, UK

Editorial Offices
The Atrium, Southern Gate, Chichester, West Sussex, PO19 8SQ, UK
9600 Garsington Road, Oxford, OX4 2DQ, UK
350 Main Street, Malden, MA 02148-5020, USA

For details of our global editorial offices, for customer services, and for information about how to apply for permission to reuse the copyright material in this book please see our website at www.wiley.com/wiley-blackwell.

Library of Congress Cataloging-in-Publication Data

Feiler, Anthony.
    Engaging 'hard to reach' parents : teacher-parent collaboration to promote children's learning / Anthony Feiler.
        p.   cm.
    Includes bibliographical references and index.
    ISBN 978-0-470-68229-6 (cloth) – ISBN 978-0-470-51632-4 (pbk.) 1. Education, Elementary–Parent participation–Great Britain.   2. Parent-teacher relationships–Great Britain.   3. Motivation in education–Great Britain.   4. Children with social disabilities–Education–Great Britain.   5. Underachievers–Great Britain.   6. Child welfare–Great Britain.   I. Title.
    LB1048.5.F45 2010
    371.19′2–dc22

                                                                        2009036648

A catalogue record for this book is available from the British Library.

Typeset in 11/13.5pt Minion by Aptara Inc., New Delhi, India.
Printed and bound in Singapore by Fabulous Printers Pte Ltd

1   2010

39.21   371,192
Fei

Contents

About the Author

Anthony Feiler is a Reader in Education at the Graduate School of Education, University of Bristol. He taught in a primary school in south east London, worked as an educational psychologist in Manchester, Wandsworth and Islington, and was a tutor on the professional training course for educational psychologists at University College London before moving to higher education. Anthony currently teaches a Masters Special/Inclusive Education course at the University of Bristol, and his research interests include teacher–parent collaboration and support strategies for disabled children. He has undertaken research in these areas funded by the DCSF, the British Academy and the Esmée Fairbairn Foundation, and is currently a researcher on a government-funded project *The 14-19 Reforms: The Centre Research Study – The Impact upon Schools and Colleges.*

Preface

This book focuses on how teachers can reach out to parents, particularly those parents who experience difficulties engaging with schools, so that collaborative links can be established to help children and young people learn and develop. Although the main emphasis is on relationships between parents and teachers, much of the content is of relevance to other professionals working with families, children and young people.

The use of the term 'parents' in this book includes all natural parents and any person or carer who may not be a natural parent but has parental responsibility for a child or young person.

The field addressed in this book complements the recent text by Pomerantz, K., Hughes, M. and Thompson, D. (2008) entitled *How to Reach 'Hard to Reach' Children: Improving Access, Participation and Outcomes*, also published by John Wiley & Sons, Ltd.

Acknowledgements

Parts of this text draw on the author's experience gained during the Home–School Knowledge Exchange (HSKE) project, a large-scale research study funded by the ESRC and conducted at the University of Bristol, 2001–2005. Sincere thanks are extended to the HSKE team: Professor Martin Hughes (project director), Dr Jane Andrews, Dr Pamela Greenhough, Leida Salway, Dr David Johnson, Vicky Stinchcombe, Jan Winter, Professor Andrew Pollard, Professor Marilyn Osborn, Wan Ching Yee and Dr Mary Scanlan. The book also draws on the author's research on the South West Autism Project. Thanks are due to this project's director, Professor Alec Webster (who provided valuable commentary on the content and structure of this book) and to Valerie Webster.

1

Introduction

This book explores one of the most imperative challenges in the field of education – how to form relationships with parents who encounter difficulties engaging with their children's school. Although this is undoubtedly a daunting task, it is a necessary one to assist children's learning and development. There are encouraging indications that the approaches currently adopted by schools to enhance collaboration with parents are becoming increasingly effective. A recent survey by the Office for Standards in Education found that all participating schools valued the involvement of parents and carers, and the majority of them were rated by inspectors from the Office for Standards in Education as good or outstanding at involving parents (Office for Standards in Education, 2007). Furthermore, research in the United Kingdom on parents' perspectives of their involvement in education has indicated that their viewpoints are broadly positive and that there has been a recent rise in parents' perceived level of involvement. Peters et al. (2008) sought parental views during a telephone survey and found that the proportion of parents who reported feeling very involved in their child's school life had significantly increased over the last few years: from 29% in 2001, 38% in 2004, to 51% in 2007. Furthermore, it was found that more parents were likely to regard

Engaging 'Hard to Reach' Parents: Teacher–Parent Collaboration to Promote Children's Learning By Anthony Feiler © 2010 John Wiley & Sons, Ltd

their child's education as primarily their responsibility (28%). This marks a change from previous years, when parents tended to view education as the school's responsibility.

Despite these encouraging indications that parents generally feel more involved in their child's school life than in the past, the difficulties and complexities that many schools face when attempting to develop effective relationships with parents can be profound. Carvalho (2001) argues that the relationship between schools and parents is often characterized by intrinsic tensions and mutual feelings of suspicion and hostility. This viewpoint is echoed in Jackson and Remillard's (2005) concern that rather than viewing parents as a source of support, schools can at times see some parents as deficits to children and as 'problems to overcome', particularly parents from low-income communities. The need to engage with parents, who for a variety of reasons might experience difficulties in accessing schools and who might be termed 'hard to reach', is undoubtedly one of the most demanding issues facing teachers in today's schools.

It should be acknowledged at the outset that the importance of schools and professionals developing productive relationships with parents has been recognized for some time. This field, traditionally referred to as 'parental involvement', was identified in the United Kingdom as an important matter for educationists in the Plowden report *Children and Their Primary Schools* (Department for Education and Science, 1967), and has since achieved increasing prominence as a priority in education policy. The Plowden report comprised a major review of primary education. It highlighted the importance of placing the child at the centre of educational practice and emphasized the key role that parents played in supporting children's learning. Aspects of this report now seem quaint and dated. For example, in Chapter 4 of the report, 'Participation by parents', there is an account of an interview with one of the participants who recommended that parents should 'know their children's teachers at least as well as they know the milkman'. However, considering that this document was written half a century ago, many of the recommendations and observations seem remarkably prescient; for example, strong support is expressed for the development of 'community schools' that provide after-school services for children, their parents and members of the locality. Furthermore, there was recognition that schools need to adopt flexibility and determination to engage some groups of parents – a theme that resonates strongly with current thinking: 'However many and pressing the invitations from school, some parents will not respond, and amongst them will be some of those whose children most need help. Should they be sought out? It would be a policy of despair to do nothing about them' (Department for Education and Science, 1967, section 113).

A decade after the Plowden report, another influential government publication was launched that later came to be regarded as a milestone in education policy making in the United Kingdom: *The report of the Committee of Enquiry into the Education of Handicapped Children and Young People*, or the *Warnock Report* (Her Majesty's Stationery Office, 1978). This review of provision for children with educational and other difficulties is now seen as a watershed in the development of contemporary perspectives and attitudes to children with special needs and their families. A full chapter is devoted to parental involvement, in which there is a great emphasis on the need for the relationship between professionals and parents to be one of partnership: '. . . the successful education of children with special educational needs is dependent upon the full involvement of their parent; indeed, unless the parents are seen as equal partners in the educational process the purpose of our report will be frustrated' (Her Majesty's Stationery Office, 1978, p. 150).

Within 20 years of the publication of the Warnock report, parental involvement in education in the United Kingdom was recognized as a core element of effective education for all children (not just those with special needs) and was attracting increasing attention from the government. Funding was secured for the 'Parental Involvement in Children's Education' (PICE) team, which produced a number of influential research reports and other publications, for example *Involving Parents, Raising Achievement* (Bastiani and White, 2003). Politicians became increasingly interested in parents' contribution to education, and at the 2000 Labour Party Conference, David Blunkett (then minister for education) announced, 'Education is a partnership in which parents have a critical role. We want them to engage much more in the education of their children than in the past. Their children need it. It can make a huge difference.' David Blunkett's words point to one of the key reasons why parents' involvement in education is now internationally viewed as a priority by governments. The 'huge difference' that David Blunkett is referring to is the potential for parents to improve children's academic achievement, and this has become an enduring theme in education policy in recent years.

Parental involvement in children's learning

Ever since the introduction of the National Curriculum in the United Kingdom during the 1990s, there has been a very strong emphasis on raising academic attainment within schools by focusing on the curriculum and teaching methods. However, interest amongst researchers and policy makers has started to shift to factors outside school that might contribute to improvements in learning, and it is increasingly being acknowledged that the support provided at home by parents and other family members can also play a crucial role in how well children perform at school. The theme of schools engaging with parents in order to improve children's learning and development has become a priority within UK educational policy, and the strength of the government's conviction that this is an important initiative is indicated in the Standards Site web page on parental involvement, where it is asserted that children will be much more likely to view school positively and be receptive to learning if they see that their parents are enthusiastic about education. It is also proposed that engaging with parents is therefore 'one of the most vital parts of providing children with an excellent education' (www.standards.dfes.gov.uk/parentalinvolvement).

The UK government's view that good parenting is essential for children's development is also evident in *Every Child Matters* (Department for Education and Skills, 2003c). In this landmark publication, the government acknowledges that parents' relationship with their children has a profound impact on their development: 'The bond between the child and their parents is the most crucial influence on a child's life. Parenting has a strong impact on a child's educational development, behaviour and mental health' (Department for Education and Skills, 2003c, p. 39). This point has been eloquently discussed by Lochrie (2004) in her report on the place of family learning. Lochrie argues that the education of children has for too long ignored the pivotal role played by children's parents and other family members. She suggests that the most effective means of helping children to learn and develop is through a continuous, respectful interchange with parents. Lochrie's proposal that professionals need to engage with parents in order to support them in their care of children is a theme that permeates UK government policy. In a statement that epitomizes the extent to which support for parents is seen as a means for enhancing children's learning and development and that engagement with parents is an imperative aspect of policy and practice, the government declares that supporting parents and carers lies at the heart of its approach to improving children's lives (Department for Education and Skills, 2003c). A core set of UK government plans for supporting parents is set out in *Every Child Matters* (Department for Education and Skills, 2003c), and these range from the development of universal services for all families to the provision of more specialist support, targeted at families considered to have particular needs. The *Every Child Matters* proposals include the following:

- **Extending universal services such as family learning programmes.** Such initiatives include the government's *Family Literacy, Language and Numeracy: A Guide for Extended Schools* which can be downloaded from the government's Teachernet website (www.teachernet.gov.uk). The aim of such materials is to help parents engage in their children's development and provide opportunities to increase family involvement in learning. For a full discussion of parent education programmes, see Nicola McGrath's chapter 'Engaging the hardest to reach parents in parenting-skills programmes', in Pomerantz et al. (2007).
- **Providing specialist parenting support.** In addition to services open to all parents, the UK government has identified a need for a range of tailor-made help and support for specific groups, for example home visiting programmes for some families with very young children.
- **Ensuring better communication between parents and schools.** This initiative involves creating more opportunities for families (especially fathers) to become more closely involved with events in school through parents' associations and school governors.
- **Developing parent education programmes.** It is intended that these are targeted at the parents of younger children aged 5–8 years, and may involve weekly sessions where parents are trained to use behaviour management techniques.

It is worth noting that whilst *Every Child Matters* addresses the needs of children in England, both the Welsh Assembly government and the Scottish government have expressed interest in this policy development. It is evident that some of the core principles that underpin the approach being adopted in England have been given similar prominence in policies developed in these countries. In the National Assembly for Wales' (2000) *Children and Young People: A Framework for Partnership*, the fundamental importance of the role played by parents is recognized. As with policy in England, it is acknowledged that whilst all parents need some help with the challenges of bringing up children, '. . . attention to the most deprived areas, where frequently the formal and informal support networks are at their weakest, is particularly beneficial in reducing disadvantage in later life' (Welsh Assembly, 2004, p. 33). Furthermore, in the Welsh Assembly's policy priorities for 2001–2010, set out in *The Learning Country* (National Assembly for Wales, 2001), the emphasis on support for families echoes that found in *Every Child Matters*: 'We aim to give every child a flying start. We seek to plant ambition and high expectation early on. We wish to support parents to enable this to happen' (National Assembly for Wales, 2001, p. 15).

The Scottish Executive (2007) in its publication *Reaching Out to Families* (www.scotland.gov.uk) presents a refreshingly positive introduction to good practice on parental involvement in Scottish schools. This document sets out key messages on building relationships with families, with a strong, unifying theme that partnership grows when parents feel respected and valued. There is also an emphasis on the importance of viewing partnership as a two-way process, which means that schools have much to learn from parents in the same way as parents have much to learn from schools; see Box 1.1 for a summary of these principles.

Box 1.1 Core principles taken from *Reaching Out to Families* (Scottish Executive, 2007).

Both school staff and parents need to see the benefit of communication

When school staff have an awareness of family background, they can find it easier to understand the issues children may be experiencing at home. Parents who recognize that professionals in school respect them and value their own views are more likely to trust professionals.

All staff are active participants in a whole school approach
Each member of staff will have current insight into the needs of the child and family – it is important to allow parents to connect with staff with whom they feel most comfortable.

Staff who understand parents' concerns and circumstances will find it easier to build relationships
Most parents will experience difficulties in their parenting at one time or another. Family circumstances can change suddenly and dramatically, whilst for some families, conflict, fragility or pressure may be more sustained.

Draw on resources within communities and families
We know that children do better when their parents support their learning. Schools may tap into community resources and other council services to draw support, for example family learning projects, specialist support and services dedicated to specific communities or identity issues.

Parents will respond to staff who show care for their children
Some parents will remember their own negative experiences of school and feel that these are replayed or reinforced when their children experience difficulties. It is important to state clearly at the beginning of a meeting that the staff have the interests of the child as their central concern and that they therefore share the same viewpoint as the parent.

Support all staff to support children better
Staff who address complex and emotive issues with families will themselves require support in order to be confident in their role, for example from senior management or peers.

The above themes have been endorsed in Scotland by the publication of *Getting It Right for Every Child* (www.scotland.gov.uk/gettingitright), a national programme that aims to incorporate new thinking and best practice for all professionals working with young people, parents and carers. A prominent feature of the approach is the building of solutions with and around children and their families in order to support a positive shift in culture, systems and practice. The model encourages practitioners to plot well-being indicators and to identify resilience and protective factors in order to make constructive plans for all children.

The Scottish Executive's key principles present a positive and constructive framework for developing relationships with parents. This is in contrast to aspects of policy in England in which a more coercive note is introduced for some parents described as hard to reach, and in which there is a focus not only on parents' needs but also on parents' responsibilities. The emphasis on parents' responsibilities has become a strongly endorsed topic in UK policy, for example: 'Some parents will be harder to engage and their problems may be more entrenched. When persisting truanting or anti-social behaviour is condoned by parents, compulsory action may be needed to ensure parents meet their responsibilities' (Department for Education and Skills, 2003c, p. 43). Crozier and Reay (2005) have expressed concern about such compulsory action, and suggest that the UK government may be adopting approaches that will not lead to equitable participation for some parents: '. . . [the] Government has never, seemingly, been convinced that parents were pulling their weight with respect to their children's education . . . we have the Anti-Social Behaviour Act (2003), to cover extended absences and truancy. In addition, we saw the introduction of parenting classes both on a voluntary basis and as a punishment for such putative misdemeanours' (Crozier and Reay, 2005, p. ix). Concerns about pressures on parents to meet their responsibilities are addressed in more detail in Chapter 6.

Parental engagement and raising standards

As mentioned above, the UK government's encouragement to schools to engage with parents stems in large part from a belief that parental involvement raises academic attainment in schools. The evidence for a link between parental involvement and educational achievement comes from a variety of sources. Desforges and Abouchaar (2003) conducted a wide-ranging review of the literature on the effect of parental involvement on children's achievement and adjustment, and examined two discrete sets of literature. One encompassed the process of **spontaneously occurring** parental involvement and its impact on children's educational outcomes. The second body of literature focused on evaluations of **interventions** designed to enhance parental involvement. Desforges' review indicates that spontaneous parental involvement is diverse and multifaceted and might include parents modelling constructive social and educational values, parent–child discussions, parents' contact with schools to share information and parents' participation in school events. Unsurprisingly, it emerged that the level and type of spontaneous parental involvement is influenced by social background factors such as mothers' own level of education, single-parent status, and the availability of material resources in the home. Another factor found to have an impact on involvement was parents' perception of their role and how confident they felt about involvement. There were indications that parental involvement diminishes as children grow older, and there is some evidence that the extent of parental engagement can be influenced by the child taking an active mediating role. Desforges notes that parenting seems to make an impact indirectly through moulding the child's self-concept as a learner and through the setting of high expectations. As for interventions to promote parental involvement, Desforges concludes that many of the evaluations of interventions are methodologically weak and that it is therefore not possible to draw firm conclusions about their efficacy in terms of influencing pupil achievement.

One of the most important findings from Desforges' review of research is that children's academic achievement and adjustment are significantly influenced by spontaneous 'at-home good parenting'. This is defined as the provision of a settled and secure home environment, an atmosphere where learning and enquiry are stimulated, plenty of parent–child conversations, parents upholding positive social and educational principles and high aspirations regarding personal fulfilment. Desforges claims that the impact of parental involvement on primary age children is very substantial – that it is greater than the impact of differences between schools, and that this occurs in families across the full range of social backgrounds and ethnic groups. A similar conclusion is reached by a research team at the University of Warwick, which has recently published a report on engaging parents in raising achievement (Harris and Goodall, 2007). These authors conclude that parental engagement is a powerful mechanism for raising student achievement in schools. Interestingly, in a similar vein to Desforges, these authors emphasized that parents have the greatest influence on the achievement of pupils through supporting their learning **in the home environment** rather than through more formal involvement in school activities.

It is worth noting that the evidence for the existence of a causal link between parental involvement and a rise in children's achievement has been questioned by some researchers. Mattingly et al. (2002) conducted a review of American studies on parent involvement programmes and considered whether such interventions are an effective means of improving student learning and other outcomes. The authors came to the same conclusion as Desforges and Abouchaar (2003): they were critical of the studies' research designs and other aspects of methodology, and concluded that the evidence for the efficacy of such programmes is lacking. Although we need to be cautious about general claims concerning parental involvement interventions and children's achievement at school, this does not mean that such initiatives are not effective – it just means that we do not yet have the evidence to prove the point. This is an exciting time to develop school–home projects, and, in later chapters, there will be discussion of a range of innovative and creative programmes that have led to improvements in children's and young people's learning, in parents' sense of self-efficacy, and in a range of other positive outcomes.

Social deprivation and 'Hard to Reach' Parents

As noted in the previous section, there is evidence that parents increasingly feel involved with their children's schools. However, in spite of the general high quality of home–school relations, many schools experience difficulties in engaging **all** parents. Barriers to parental involvement may be particularly marked in areas characterized by deprivation. In a wide-ranging review of schools in economically disadvantaged areas, Muijs et al. (2004) comment that such schools often have levels of performance that do not match national averages and may not be well positioned to encourage parents to be strongly involved in their children's education. A key challenge for teachers working in schools in disadvantaged areas is to recognize and value the diversity represented in the families they serve, for there is a danger that school policies for involving parents can be based on notions of 'model' families and may not take full account of cultural, linguistic and other barriers to involvement (Carpentier and Lall, 2005).

These issues are increasingly acknowledged by policy makers in the United Kingdom. The government's report *Support for Parents: Best Start for Children* (Department for Education and Skills, 2005b) asserts that as some parents have greater needs and face greater challenges than others, it is important to provide more support for those who need it most. There is an acknowledgment of the importance of targeting families living in the most disadvantaged areas, and to put in place preventive strategies to tackle so-called 'cycles of deprivation' in order to prevent an intergenerational transmission of difficulties. In its publication *Aiming High for Children: Support for Families* (Department for Education and Skills, 2007), there is a similarly strong focus on the need for service providers to make themselves more accessible to vulnerable or excluded groups, including 'hard to reach' parents. Building resilience in children is viewed as a priority, and it is suggested that effective parenting is a key protective factor in the development of such resilience. In this document, the government again emphasizes that schools and other public services need to reach out to families who need them most, and the extended schools programme from the *Every Child Matters* agenda is viewed as a key initiative to achieve this goal.

The acknowledgement that collaboration with parents may be particularly difficult in areas characterized by deprivation chimes with a feature of medical service delivery that has become known as the inverse care law. First described by Julian Tudor Hart (1971), the inverse care law declares that the availability of good medical care tends to vary inversely with the needs of the population served, and that those living in poorer areas with greater health needs are apt to receive worse medical provision. In other words, those who need health care most are least likely to receive it. It is probable that the inverse care law is not confined to medical practice and may be a feature of a range of services, including education. An indication that such a process may be in operation comes from the work of a number of researchers who have noted that parental involvement is strongly influenced by social background factors and that engagement with schools tends to be much lower amongst groups living in deprived conditions (e.g. Desforges and Abouchaar, 2003). Parents living in areas marked by social deprivation and who are viewed as 'hard to reach' are typically those who might gain most from closer collaboration with schools.

However, terminology in this field can be problematic, and descriptors such as 'hard to reach' and 'difficult to engage' have started to be criticized. There is apprehension that such expressions can lead to deficit-centred ways of viewing some groups. Barton et al. (2004) investigated parental involvement in urban schools located in areas of high poverty in the United States and explored parents' perspectives about their engagement with education. These authors are critical of the predominance of deficit models in the literature, and the way that parents tend to be portrayed in research studies as 'subjects' to be controlled, lacking in agency and power.

RESEARCH QUOTATION

'Deficit models for understanding parents and education position parents as subjects to be manipulated ... They neither take into account the networks of individuals and resources that frame participation in scope, focus, and purpose, nor the unique experiences that frame the parents' beliefs and forge parental capital.'

Barton et al., 2004, p. 4

A similar concern about deficit approaches to families has been raised in the United Kingdom by Dyson and Robson (1999). They reviewed over 300 publications on the effectiveness and effects of school–family–community links. A key critique highlighted by these authors is that parental engagement initiatives may undermine or overlook families' practices and values, and may impose school values on communities, thereby marginalizing some families even further. Evidence that deficit-centred perspectives may still influence aspects of professional practice comes from the work of Schmidt Neven (2008). She conducted research with a range of professionals working with children and families and found that they often adopted a predominantly pathological outlook - parents tend to be blamed for their children's problems. A general concern is that schools and other agencies may overlook the diversity and richness that typify groups from different backgrounds, and terminology such as 'hard to reach' may subtly contribute to such deficit-centred outlooks.

Another problem with the term 'hard to reach' is that a focus on family-related deficits diverts attention from an examination of structural and other barriers that some families experience when trying to become involved in education. As mentioned above, there is currently interest amongst both researchers and policy makers in the United Kingdom regarding the concept of resilience in children and young people. Conventionally, resilience has been considered as a characteristic or trait that is an individual-related aspect of personality. Recent research exploring the development of psychological well-being and resilience highlights the need not only to examine *individual* factors such as personal skills and attitudes, but also the importance of studying *external* factors that act as protective processes for children and young people (such as reducing bullying in schools) (Roffey et al., 2008). It is encouraging that there is a focus not only on individuals' coping skills but also on social-environmental factors. The point is that where there are difficulties – children struggling to develop resilience, or parents finding it hard to engage with schools – it is important that there is scrutiny of structural/societal barriers that might be playing a part, not just factors operating at the individual level.

Overarching theoretical approach

This is an appropriate place to present a set of ideas that form the foundation for much of the focus of this book. This underpinning comprises two theoretical stances, which together provide a conceptual framework that will help to stitch together a range of different initiatives and research projects that are discussed in later chapters.

The first underlying construct is **sociocultural theory**. This framework for understanding human development and learning draws extensively on the work of Lev Vygotsky, who emphasized the social, interactive nature of children's development and the importance of social contexts for learning. Vygotsky's theories highlighted the part played by more knowledgeable others in directly supporting the learning process, and he argued that parents and carers, older or more experienced children, teachers and other adults play very important roles in supporting and scaffolding children's learning. For Vygotsky, the quality of support provided by more competent others is crucial.

Rogoff has developed this conception of learning as a collaborative enterprise, proposing that children's development can be viewed as a form of 'guided participation', where the child or young person stays close to a trusted guide, pays attention to the guide's actions, joins in whenever possible, and responds to any coaching that is offered (Rogoff, 1991). The implications for practitioners, researchers and parents that flow from this conceptualization include the following:

- Children's development cannot be separated from the contexts in which it occurs.
- It is important to understand children and families in authentic home or school settings, accepting that conditions and environments in which people live, play and work are often unpredictable, sometimes fraught, always complex.
- A key challenge for researchers working in these social contexts is to find ways of capturing relevant data without oversimplifying, bearing in mind how intricate, typically, are the dynamics of family or classroom and interactions between the two.
- Children's development tends to stem from 'guided participation'. Effective learning often occurs when adults scaffold children's thinking and learning in social contexts, focusing on joint problem-solving, and where adults both at home and at school have an important role, especially if they work together.
- Values are generally passed from generation to generation, and cultural differences between families are inevitable. Teachers and other professionals need to be wary when engaging with specific cultural contexts of jumping to conclusions about the inherence or hegemony of certain values, and open to others' ways of conducting their lives and bringing up children – ways that may seem unfamiliar and strange.

The professionals who developed the research projects presented in this book recognize that learning is much more than the didactic transmission of information, more than the mere conveyance of knowledge from adult to child. All these initiatives reflect elements of sociocultural theory, underlining the crucial role played by teachers, family members and others in scaffolding children's and young people's learning.

The second key theoretical stance that underpins this book is the notion of **social capital**. This is one of the most powerful conceptual foundations for understanding differences between families' capacity to become engaged in their children's education. It is worth noting that the concept of social capital has been interpreted in alternative ways by different writers, and there is not always consensus about what this term means. Ball (2003) has expressed concern about the lack of clarity in terminology in this field, commenting that differing kinds of social capital have been proposed, and that, at times, these proposed forms overlap and seem similar. However, in his book *Bowling Alone* (2000), Robert Putnam presents an authoritative account of the decline of community activity in US society which includes a detailed examination of the notion of social capital. In Putnam's analysis, social capital refers to the connections and social relations that individuals develop – contacts that result in mutual support and co-operation, making our lives more productive and providing benefits that promote our personal interests. These social linkages might span a continuum – from neighbourliness and membership of informal networks such as a walking group to the professional connections we develop at work and membership of more formal associations such as a ten-pin bowling league.

Putnam makes an important distinction between **bonding** and **bridging** social capital. Bonding social capital is inward looking, tends to lead to exclusivity, and results in tight-knit groups characterized by sameness and uniformity. Examples might include a church-based reading group for women, or contacts made at a stylish country club. Bridging networks, on the other hand, are more inclusive, tend to be outward looking and involve heterogeneous groupings of people from diverse social contexts. Bridging contacts are often loose-knit and comprise 'weak' ties and relationships (Ball, 2003). Such contacts can provide important opportunities for individuals seeking information or advancement. Examples of bridging social capital might include the civil rights movement in the United States, the form of connections that are developed in the United Kingdom by parents in primary schools when waiting for their children in the playground, or a wide network of contacts and potential contacts that some families develop (e.g. through acquaintances of relatives). The important point here is that both forms of social capital, bonding and bridging, can provide families with advantages. As the old adage has it, what matters most is not **what** you know but **who** you know. For parents who might be unsure about how the education system works, being able to contact a relative or friend who is a teacher or education professional may provide valuable information about how to approach staff at their child's school.

A third form of social capital has been proposed, and this is the notion of **cultural** capital, developed by Pierre Bourdieu, a French sociologist. Bordieu was interested in why educational outcomes for children from different families can vary so dramatically. He argued that these variations are to a large extent explained in terms of differing levels of cultural capital, which includes the values and outlooks that we pick up from our background and culture, bequeathed to us usually by our families through a process of socialization. Cultural capital may be embodied in a certain way of speaking, or may be reflected in our educational experiences and qualifications. Of course, all children have cultural experiences, but some cultural experiences (e.g. exposure to certain linguistic structures and familiarity with certain learning opportunities) may be more 'valuable' than others as they mesh in more closely with schools' curricula and teaching methods. Lareau (2000) provides an astute analysis of the mechanisms whereby social background can provide a pervasive and powerful advantage for some children. She argues that cultural experiences in children's homes differentially facilitate children's adjustment to school and academic achievement, and this process **transforms** aspects of family life or cultural resources into cultural capital. This mechanism results in children from poorer backgrounds being differentially disadvantaged, as their cultural resources may be of less value to the school. Some parents will deliberately put their cultural capital to use by coaching their children at home, ensuring that their children succeed in school tests, contributing to the process whereby social advantage is passed from generation to generation. Such parents' educational experiences and successes may help them to approach teachers with more confidence and self-belief. In contrast, although parents from poorer backgrounds share middle-class parents' aspirations and want their children to do well at school, they may lack confidence in this area.

RESEARCH QUOTATION

'The working-class parents Lareau interviewed believed that they should leave academic matters to their children's teachers. Often intimidated by teachers' professional authority, these parents fear teaching their children the wrong things or instructing them in the wrong way. They see home and school as separate spheres.'

Wrigley, 2000, p. viii

As with sociocultural theory, important implications for teachers and other professionals working with parents flow from the concept of social capital theory:

- It is likely that parents will work through any difficulties they may encounter more effectively when their reserves of social capital are high and linkages to other groups are facilitated. Such connections should contribute to the quick flow of information and guidance through the maze of provision available from Local Authorities. Parents' social capital (e.g. the connections they have established and the resulting knowledge and insights they acquire) will necessitate the development of flexible services that change with parents' needs over time.
- Bonding social capital and cultural capital are arguably the most powerful factors in explaining many of the differences between diverse families' engagement with education and their capacity for overcoming challenges and obstacles. These processes result in some families being markedly disadvantaged when engaging with schools and when providing support for their children's education. Parents whose own educational experiences are limited may face considerable difficulties when approaching schools. Their sense of self-confidence in educational matters may be low, and they may have fewer resources upon which to draw in terms of know-how and social contacts.

The constructs of social and cultural capital are particularly helpful in understanding why some parents might come to be viewed as hard to reach, and some of the projects presented in this book have a deliberate focus on enhancing or building on families' social or cultural capital. The above theoretical framework will be revisited in later chapters, and will provide threads of continuity across initiatives that have been developed by different professionals from different contexts working with diverse family groups.

Concluding comments and organization of the book

The importance of parents' involvement in education has been increasingly recognized in the United Kingdom since the 1960s. Currently, there is strong support for parental involvement in England,

Wales and Scotland partly because of the conviction that this will lead to improved learning outcomes for children and young people. It is increasingly recognized that deficit models that imply that there is something 'wrong' with certain families are unhelpful for establishing trusting partnerships between professionals and parents.

The remainder of this book is organized in the following manner. In Chapter 2, various characterizations of 'hard to reach' parents will be discussed, and there will be an exploration of reasons why some parents seem to find it so challenging to engage with schools. The next three chapters proceed from macro to micro issues in the field of parental engagement: Chapter 3 considers international studies on school–home links; Chapter 4 presents promising practice from the United Kingdom; and Chapter 5 presents a more finely focused analysis of small-scale initiatives that have involved home visiting as a means of engaging with parents. Aspects of parental involvement initiatives can be controversial and have attracted criticism within the academic community, particularly debates surrounding the conceptualization of parents being 'hard to reach' – Chapter 6 examines some of the core concerns that have been voiced. The book concludes with commentary in Chapter 7 on lessons learned and how schools can make themselves more open and approachable to parents.

2

Types of Engagement, Explanations and Risk Factors

Introduction

Parents' engagement with school and education is multi-faceted and complex. This is partly due to the fact that parental actions that might be termed 'involvement in education' are numerous and wide ranging. Parental involvement can vary extensively in terms of both its manner and what motivates it. For example, parents may contribute at a general level to school proceedings such as school fairs and fund-raising events; or they may spend time at home focusing on helping their child with homework. Although both could be described as involvement in education, there appears to be a marked difference between parents supporting the school and parents helping their own child. However, another level of complexity can emerge, as distinctions that may initially appear straightforward can often, on closer scrutiny, become blurred. For example, Russell and Granville (2005) conducted research into parents' views about parental involvement in education in Scotland and found that a core reason for some parents volunteering to help out in school was to become more acquainted with the school's functioning and procedures in order to be better

Engaging 'Hard to Reach' Parents: Teacher–Parent Collaboration to Promote Children's Learning By Anthony Feiler © 2010 John Wiley & Sons, Ltd

positioned to help their child. The motive underlying parents' willingness to help with school events may well be similar to reasons why parents help their child at home – both enhance their capacity to support their own child's learning. Thus, in order to make sense of parents' involvement, we may need to pay attention not only to what it looks like, but also to what motivates it.

In this chapter, the intricate nature of parental involvement is examined, and various characterizations of so-called 'hard to reach' parents are considered:

- The chapter starts with an exploration of the nature of 'parental involvement', and we examine social and historical factors that have contributed to the exclusion of certain groups.
- We discuss the alleged 'cycle of deprivation' – the proposition that disadvantage tends to be handed down inexorably from one generation to the next, undermining the capacity of certain groups to cut loose from poverty and its consequences.
- On a more positive note, we then examine the proposition that all families have resources of cultural and social capital that can contribute to children's learning and development.
- This is followed by commentary on parents' engagement with school events, and their involvement in less visible forms of support at home.
- The remainder of the chapter considers a range of risk factors that might result in some parents being viewed as 'hard to reach'.

Before considering the field of literature on parental engagement, it is worth noting that a large number of studies on parental involvement foreground the perspectives of mothers, not fathers. The commentary that follows reflects this partiality, but is not intended to imply that fathers' involvement does not matter. Investigators generally develop contacts with mothers when conducting educational research investigations, and this can result in an under-reporting of fathers' viewpoints. The following quotation from the Department for Education and Skills (2004b) booklet *Engaging Fathers: Involving Parents, Raising Achievement* attests to the importance of fathers' roles:

RESEARCH QUOTATION

'*Research shows that both fathers and mothers impact on their children's development ... Taking action to include both parents in the life of the school and in their children's learning can make a significant and positive difference to children's achievements, motivation and self-esteem.*'

Department for Education and Skills, 2004b, p. 2

Exclusion and marginalization: social and historical factors

In a major review of the literature on exclusion amongst children aged 0–13 and their families, Buchanan et al. (2004) acknowledge that the term 'social exclusion' is open to different interpretations and is still developing. Nevertheless, there is a close link between notions of the 'socially excluded' and groups who might be described as 'hard to reach', and Buchanan et al. identify core factors that are associated with risks of families becoming marginalized. A selection is presented in Box 2.1.

Box 2.1   Factors associated with a risk of social exclusion for children aged 0–13 and their families (taken from Buchanan et al., 2004).

- **Poor living standards.** There are strong links between child poverty (defined as low income and poor living standards) and short- and long-term outcomes for children, including poor achievement at school and unsettled behaviour.
- **Poor housing conditions.** Housing that is overcrowded and in a poor condition is associated with children's ill health, educational disadvantage and slower social development. Children from minority ethnic groups and disabled children are more likely to live in poor housing conditions.

(continued)

- **Disabled children and children with special educational needs.** Families with a disabled child are more likely to experience poverty. It has been estimated that it costs up to three times as much to bring up a child with severe impairments as a non-disabled child.
- **Lack of access to high-quality early years provision.** Research indicates that the provision of good-quality nurseries and other forms of preschool provision has a positive impact on children's development, and an additional benefit is that early years services help parents to take up employment and avoid the risk of family poverty.
- **Poor health.** Ill health may not necessarily lead to social exclusion for children and families. However, there are clear indications that material deprivation can result in poor health. So poor health in a family may be an indicator of other stressors such as poverty and poor living standards.
- **Access to justice.** Families experiencing debt, unemployment, discrimination, mental health problems and family breakdown may be particularly at risk of being socially excluded – such problems might be avoided if parents have appropriate legal advice or access to legal services.

Welshman (2006a) presents a penetrating and perceptive scrutiny of conceptions of excluded groups, and of concerns about the existence of an 'underclass' in society over the past 120 years or so. His analysis provides a useful context for the current focus on so-called 'hard to reach parents', and reminds us that historical and social factors can play a significant role in the development and use of such terms:

The 'social residuum' (1880s). In the 1880s, the notion of a social residuum served to distinguish between the respectable working-class and the lowest section of society, that is, a different and separate group or class. Another term closely allied to the 'social residuum' was 'the undeserving poor'. This dates back to the seventeenth-century 'Poor Law' in England (the 1601 Poor Relief Act), when a system of parish-scale social security

funding was introduced and local magistrates needed to identify claimants whose applications were judged to be justified. A
distinction was drawn between the 'deserving' and 'undeserving
poor'.

The 'unemployable' (1900s). During the early 1900s there were
concerns about the growing number of adults deemed to be
unemployable. Some regarded this group to comprise those who
were unwilling and those who for various reasons were unable to
work. The full employment that occurred during the First World
War later served to reduce the focus on a supposed 'underclass'
that was unemployable.

The 'social problem group' (1920s). During the 1920s and 1930s,
fears about 'mental defectiveness' and the notion that this condition could be passed from one generation to the next resulted in
the creation of the so-called social problem group. During this
period, the Eugenics movement exerted a strong influence on
social policy debates, proposing that through selective breeding
and social engineering society should encourage the most able
and healthy to produce more children and the least able to have
fewer children.

The 'problem family' (1950s). The Eugenics movement's focus
on social problem groups became discredited when it was associated with the Nazi atrocities of the 1930s. By the 1940s, the
notion of the social problem group began to be superseded by
a new conceptualization of the underclass: the problem family. This conceptualization was partly triggered by the evacua-
tion of families from cities during the early years of the Second
World War, when the poor health and living standards experienced by some city families became more visible. Official and
other reports from this period refer to the neglect of children
living in dirty, disordered conditions, and the deployment of
health visitors was advocated to provide practical help in the
home.

The 'underclass' (1980s). In Britain and in the United States during the 1970s and 1980s, there began to be a shift in the type of
questions probing why some families experienced problems. Unlike the previous deficit approach that blamed families, debates
were held about disadvantage resulting from systemic problems
in society. In the United Kingdom, the term 'underclass' was
used to characterize groups of people affected by poverty who

experienced long-term unemployment. However, one of the problems with the term underclass was that it was applied to a wide range of different groups – such as certain migrant workers, minority ethnic groups, and communities where there were high levels of crime and state dependency. There was little consensus amongst researchers or policy makers about definitions, and by the mid-1990s, a new description became favoured.

The socially excluded (1990s). The concept of social exclusion was first used by sociologists in France in the 1970s. It was applied to people living on the margins of society in run-down estates on the edge of cities with limited access to social amenities.

A conceptualization that could be added to the above list is the focus of this book – the notion of 'hard to reach parents'. In the government publication *Reaching Out* (Cabinet Office, 2006), the government refers to the persistent and deep-seated exclusion of a small minority, which stands out starkly in comparison with the lifestyles of the more affluent:

RESEARCH QUOTATION

'The disadvantages these individuals face are usually apparent early in life and can persist long into adulthood and old age ... It has become clearer that there are small groups of people whose needs are unique and complex and who are particularly difficult to reach. Highly localised and tailored responses will be needed to extend the opportunities enjoyed by most people to those suffering the effects of social exclusion.'

Cabinet Office, 2006, p. 10

Welshman's (2006a) historical overview of conceptions of an 'underclass' illustrates starkly that the terminology used to describe those who might be considered socially excluded or difficult to reach is influenced by historical, social and political developments. The nineteenth-century descriptor 'social residuum' seems dated and condemnatory with its connotations of deficit and inadequacy. Today, we tend to be wary of explanations about others' social conditions and lifestyles that imply that families alone can be held accountable for the difficulties they face. Welshman's analysis acts as a reminder that the labels used to describe groups in society need to be treated cautiously and critically, and that terms such as 'socially excluded' and 'hard to reach' are socially constructed. These terms are created by writers and policy makers attempting to make sense of human activities by identifying patterns and regularities in human behaviour. They are not immutable, clinical or scientific categories. They are descriptive in nature, not explanatory, and there is a worrying sense of circularity about the way such phrases are used, as exemplified in the following:

Question: Why do some families experience persistent and deep-seated problems?

Answer: Because they are members of the underclass.

Question: How do we know such families are members of the underclass?

Answer: Because they experience persistent and deep-seated problems.

Terms such as the 'underclass', the 'socially excluded' and the 'hard to reach' offer little to elucidate **why** some families experience entrenched and unrelenting difficulties. Various writers have proposed different theoretical frameworks for exploring the mechanisms that might play a part in the process whereby some parents become marginalized and are then viewed as hard to reach. These proposed mechanisms range from social process models that examine factors within society that perpetuate poverty and disadvantage to individualized models that focus on the experiences of those involved and the way that parents' confidence and self-belief can be eroded when meeting teachers and other professionals. Each of these frameworks has different implications for action by schools.

The notion of an intergenerational cycle of deprivation

In this section, we explore models that account for differing levels of parents' involvement in their children's education.

Welshman (2006b) discusses two of the major perspectives that examine why certain groups in society are excluded – individual explanations and structural (or external) explanations – and notes that these are oppositional in nature. Individual explanations propose that those with poor living standards are characterized by inadequacies of their own making that result in a sub-culture of poverty. One of the most striking early examples was the Victorian concept of the undeserving poor (referred to above), and the suggestion that those living in poverty are themselves to blame for their circumstances and are, therefore, not worthy of handouts from society. In contrast, more recent conceptualizations emphasize structural factors in society that may result in certain groups becoming socially excluded from services and employment opportunities, factors such as language barriers, or the tendency for some schools to over-rely on written English when communicating with parents.

An idea that has dominated social policy for the last few decades is the proposition that a cycle of deprivation operates that causes disadvantage to be passed from one generation to the next and prevents certain groups breaking free from extreme poverty and exclusion. According to Coffield et al. (1980), one of the earliest references to the idea of a cycle of deprivation was presented in a book by Jamieson Hurry published in 1921 entitled *Poverty and Its Vicious Circles*. However, it was not until the mid-twentieth century that this theory began to have a significant impact on educational provision. When Lyndon Johnson took over the US presidency after the assassination of John Kennedy in 1963, he stated that social deprivation was the most pressing domestic problem facing the country and declared a 'war on poverty'. Soon afterwards the *Head Start* programme was set up in the United States (in 1965), and it remains to this day an immense, state-funded scheme that supports a range of education, health, nutrition, and parent involvement services for low-income children and their families. To illustrate the remarkable scope of this initiative, in 2007 a sum of over US$6.5 billion was allocated in the United States to 1600 programmes involving over 900,000 children. The principal rationale underpinning the development of the *Head Start* programme was that this initiative might weaken the so-called 'culture of poverty' (O'Connor, 2003).

The conception of a culture of poverty is not confined to the United States – it underpins aspects of UK government policy on engaging hard to reach parents and is linked to an alleged cycle of disadvantage:

RESEARCH QUOTATION

'We know that children born into disadvantaged households have a higher chance of experiencing similar problems to their parents – this is known as the inter-generational cycle of disadvantage. It is a pattern seen across many of the most at-risk groups in our society, including teenage parents, children in care, those with poor educational attainment and those engaging in anti-social behaviour and offending.'

Cabinet Office, 2006, p. 18

The notion of a cycle of disadvantage suggests that being born into a low-income household impacts severely on a child's life chances, and one of the objectives of the UK government's *Sure Start* programme was to break this supposed sequence and prevent the development of a self-replicating 'underclass'. Concerns about intergenerational poverty resulted in government-directed initiatives to address specific aspects of children's learning, and the *Basic Skills Agency* with its programmes to support family literacy was in the vanguard of this initiative (The National Literacy Trust, 2001).

Although intervention might aim to interrupt the supposed cycle of deprivation at any stage – for example, by improving housing, or by preventing family breakdown – a dominant theme in policy publications in both the United States and the United Kingdom is that tackling the alleged intergenerational transmission of difficulties might be best achieved through early intervention strategies that improve young children's preschool and school experiences. For example, D'Addio (2007) suggested: '. . . getting good quality care in early childhood, pre-school and school is the essential tool for promoting intergenerational mobility.' The *Head Start* programme in the United States influenced the subsequent development of the *Sure Start* programme in the United Kingdom, both of which laid the same emphasis on early intervention for young children. Policy makers judged that effective support in the earliest years offered the greatest potential for reducing social exclusion, and Glass (1999) noted that there was agreement that *Sure Start* early intervention schemes should, where possible, share a set of core characteristics and be:

- Two-generational (involve parents as well as children).
- Non-stigmatizing (avoid labelling 'problem families').
- Multi-faceted (target a range of factors; e.g. not just education, or health, or 'parenting').
- Persistent (last long enough to make a real difference).
- Locally driven (i.e. based on consultation and involvement of parents and local communities).
- Culturally appropriate and sensitive to the needs of children and parents.

It should be emphasized that there have been critiques of the notion of a cycle of disadvantage and concerns have been raised that this concept has been overemphasized in debates about the persistence of poverty (see Welshman, in press, for commentary on this field).

So far, the discussion of factors that might account for differing levels of parents' involvement in their children's education tends to reflect the view that 'society knows best' and that there are some families who need help or intervention because what they do is somehow lacking or substandard. A growing stance within the general field of early intervention is that support schemes should not be deficit focused, developed on the premise that some parents lack the knowledge or skills that other families possess. Linked to this is the contention that families have 'funds' of abilities and resources that are too often overlooked by professionals offering interventionist support – abilities and skills that need to be recognized and built upon.

Cultural and social capital, parental agency and families' funds of knowledge

As discussed in Chapter 1, one of the most frequently cited theories exploring families' knowledge, capacities and social connections is the notion of cultural and social capital. This conceptualization has much to offer when analysing parents' markedly differing levels of engagement with education. Cultural capital encompasses the varying outlooks and values that parents and other carers inculcate in children (Bourdieu, 1986), and it tends to be reflected in the range of artefacts that can be found in homes, for example novels, non-fiction books and computers. Cultural capital is also reflected in family members' educational qualifications. Bourdieu holds that cultural capital is transmitted from parents to children unconsciously and swiftly throughout the period when children are raised and socialized. For example, some parents may instil in children an interest in narrative and storybooks during the preschool years, thus providing a strong foundation for literacy learning when the child first starts school. Social capital, on the other hand, refers to the set of contacts and connections that families build up – the complex system of associations and mutual acquaintances that are a part of families' community and wider networks. Social capital is the product of families investing time and energy in establishing social relationships that are directly usable in the short or long term.

Ball (2003) comments that families' social and cultural capital can combine in various ways and can help families to make sense of and manage systems at school. For example, parents who have teachers amongst their family or friendship groups may know more about how literacy is taught, or how schools organize homework. A crucial point here is that parents from poorer backgrounds tend to be at a disadvantage when interacting with teachers as they may have less knowledge to make sense of systems at school and may lack the management skills to deal with these. In a detailed and compelling study, Lareau (2000) describes research conducted in two elementary schools in the United States with contrasting intakes of working-class and middle-class children. She notes the dramatic difference in the way working and middle-class parents interact with the schools: in middle-class families, relationships between parents and teachers were characterized by interconnectedness (e.g. parents confidently entering the school corridors and holding conversations with staff, and visiting classrooms), whereas in working-class families such relationships were typified by distance or separation. Lareau explores in depth how parents' occupational status seems to be associated with their styles of interaction when talking with teachers. She found that the working-class parents tended to exhibit feelings of dependence, passivity and insecurity with teachers. A lack of confidence in their ability to understand, challenge and face teachers as equals impacted strongly on these parents. Lareau proposes that dissimilarities between working- and middle-class parents are not about differences in how much parents value education – she argues that both value it equally strongly; nor (she suggests) are these differences about teachers at the two schools interacting differently with the parents. In her research in the two schools, Lareau found that both sets of teachers generally made the same requests for parental involvement. Lareau argues that key to understanding the different patterns of parental engagement in the two schools is the recognition that the two sets of parents have differing types of resources and outlooks, which in turn shape their behaviour, that is, differing levels of social and cultural capital.

A factor that is closely linked to the concept of cultural and social capital and that might help explain variations in the extent to which parents engage with schools has been termed 'parental agency'. Vincent (2001) explored the interrelationship between social class and parents' sense of self-assurance and 'agency'. She examined parents' roles in secondary education and contrasted the degree to which parents from middle and working-class backgrounds felt confident in giving voice to their views about education. Vincent focused on parents' differing levels of intensity of involvement at school and grouped the parents under three headings:

- **High involvement** parents were those who attended meetings in addition to parents' evenings, and/or who initiated interaction with the school. Some of the parents characterized in this manner demonstrated considerable knowledge about education, mostly stemming from parents' employment in education or related occupations.
- **Intermediate involvement** parents were those who usually attended parents' evenings and had perhaps one or two other instances of interaction with the school, not necessarily initiated by themselves. They did not generally attend other meetings.
- **Low involvement** parents may have attended parents' evenings but otherwise had minimal contact with the school, unless this was initiated by teachers.

Vincent concluded that a vital determining factor in such differing levels of parental involvement is social background: '. . . middle-class parents can call upon resources of social, cultural and economic capital in order to exercise their voice over education issues. Working-class parents, often lacking a sense of entitlement to act, and often the same degree of knowledge of the education system are more likely to be dependent upon professionals' (Vincent, 2001, p. 360).

Vincent's typology links to the work of Hoover-Dempsey and Sandler (1997). These authors proposed that three major constructs account for differing levels of parental involvement in education. First, **parents' role construction,** which refers to parental beliefs about what they are expected to accomplish in their children's education. This influences the basic range of activities that parents understand to be important for their children. Parental beliefs about role construction are viewed by the authors as particularly important in driving subsequent involvement practices. Second, **parents' sense of efficacy** for helping their children succeed in school, which focuses on the extent to which parents believe that through their involvement they are in a position to exert a positive influence on their children's educational outcomes. Third, **general requests, demands, and opportunities for involvement,** which refer to parents' perceptions that their child and his or her school actually **want** them to be involved. Factors that may contribute to parental perceptions that their involvement is valued are a child's explicit affirmation of the importance of parental participation, a school ethos that is intentionally inviting, or teachers' actions that are overtly welcoming and facilitating. The authors warn that even well-designed school programmes that actively invite parental involvement may meet with only limited success if they do not address the other core issues of parental role construction and parents' sense of efficacy for helping children succeed in school.

Parents' sense of confidence and their self-belief are clearly at the heart of successful engagement approaches. So too is the explicit recognition by teachers and other professionals that families possess important skills and abilities. Moll et al. (1992) conducted a study involving Mexican communities in Arizona, focusing on the specialist knowledge developed by families. The term 'funds of knowledge' was used to refer to historically accumulated and culturally developed bodies of knowledge and skills essential for household or individual functioning and well-being. The authors were interested in exploring how household members used their funds of knowledge to deal with changing, and often difficult, social and economic circumstances. Examples of funds of knowledge in children's households included specialist knowledge of crop planting, animal management skills, employment laws, childcare and cooking. One of the key findings from Moll et al.'s research was that families possess plentiful skills and depths of knowledge that can be overlooked by teachers:

> **RESEARCH QUOTATION**
>
> '... *our analysis of funds of knowledge represents a positive ... view of households as containing ample cultural and cognitive resources with great potential utility for classroom instruction. This ... contrasts sharply with prevailing and accepted perceptions of working-class families as somehow disorganized socially and deficient intellectually.*'
>
> **Moll et al., 1992, p. 134**

Helping parents to believe in their capacity to help their child is at the heart of Moll et al.'s research. It is possible that if schools took active steps to identify the range of interests and skills possessed by family members, and incorporated aspects of these into the curriculum and into school events, then parents' sense of self-assurance and their confidence about contributing to their child's learning could be enhanced.

Parents' involvement with school events and with their own child

In this section, we examine different **types** of family engagement with education, starting with parents' involvement in school activities. In Williams et al.'s (2002) telephone survey of families with children attending primary and secondary schools, parents were asked about the extent to which they were generally involved in activities such as helping out in class and supporting fund-raising events. Table 2.1 summarizes some of the key findings from this study.

Williams et al.'s findings suggest that there are marked differences between parents in terms of their involvement with school activities. Approximately 80% of the parents in the study had taken part in one or more of the activities listed in Table 2.1. By contrast, 20%

Table 2.1 Parents' involvement in primary and secondary school events (from Williams et al., 2002).

	Parents indicating frequent involvement, i.e. 'whenever there is an opportunity' (%)	Parents indicating involvement sometimes (%)
Helping out in class	9	12
Helping out elsewhere in school (e.g. in the library, dinner duties and school trips)	15	18
Helping with fund-raising activities	30	39
Helping with special interest groups such as sports or drama clubs	10	12
Involvement in the school's Parent Teacher Association	13	16

of the parents stated that they had **never** been involved in any such events.

In another study on parental perspectives, Russell and Granville (2005) conducted research in Scotland on parental views about involvement with education. The participating parents had children at different stages in the education system, ranging from preschool children to young people aged 19 who had recently left school. Diverse groups of parents took part in this study, representing different parental ages, types of family composition (e.g. single parent, only child, etc.), socio-economic group and geographical area (urban and rural). The authors found that patterns of parental involvement are influenced by the following factors: the age and stage of children's schooling (parents' involvement in school activities reduces significantly when children transfer to secondary school); time and effort (parents are more likely to get involved in school activities where there are fewer demands in terms of commitment and input); child persuasion (parents reported that younger children in particular can exert considerable influence when asking them to attend school events); and perceived benefit for their own child. This last factor – parental calculations as to the possible advantage for their child – is identified as a key driver of parental involvement.

As noted above, the pattern of parental involvement in children's education is strongly affected by the age of the child and the stage of schooling. Russell and Granville comment that this is partly affected by the needs of children as they make their way through school, for when children are younger, parents naturally wish to know about their learning and about their social relationships at school. Furthermore, there tend to be more opportunities for parents to forge links with staff at primary schools, particularly when parents are able to accompany their child in the classroom at the start or end of the school day. However, when children start secondary school, the ethos can change: Russell and Granville (2005) report on parents' comments about there being generally fewer opportunities for involvement. Although we know that parental involvement tends to diminish as children get older, it is unclear whether this is due to parenting and family issues, to a different ethos or structural factors in secondary schools, or a combination of both. However, there is a strong message from recent research into parents' role that a reduction in parental involvement at the secondary stage should not necessarily be interpreted as a lack of interest – parents may have fewer contacts with secondary schools because they may feel less confident about how to support their children's learning as they grow older (Carpenter and Lall, 2005; Hill and Taylor, 2004).

In addition to parents' general engagement with school, parents' involvement can be strongly focused on their own child's education. This might entail liaising with teachers and other forms of direct contact, for example parents talking to a class or subject teacher about a particular aspect of the curriculum such as a class topic or project. Another example of such engagement is attendance at parents' evenings. Organizing effective parents' evenings can be particularly challenging in secondary schools; Power and Clark's research (2000) found that parents were critical of the organization of such events, with many reporting that they found these to be frustrating and unproductive encounters. This was mentioned in particular by parents with little or no knowledge of English and by those whose children had difficulties at school. The web site on the government's standards on parents' evenings (www.standards.dfes.gov.uk) suggests that despite the challenges involved, parents' evenings are one of the best opportunities teachers have to communicate with parents and enlist their help in motivating and educating children. The following advice is offered:

- When organizing a parents' evening, consider what is hoped to be achieved and work backwards from there.
- Parents' evenings are a two-way process. Whilst parents need to know how their child is doing, there is also an opportunity for teachers to learn how the pupil behaves at home.
- Where possible, it is best to have the evening towards the beginning of the year. This allows teachers to tell parents about what will happen during the year and gain their help in resolving any problems the pupil is having at school.

In addition to involvement in more formal events such as school-based parents' evenings, by far the most common form of parents' involvement with their own child's learning takes place at home. This might comprise focused, active support such as listening to children read, preparing for school tests and helping with homework. Hughes and Greenhough (2003) conducted research into secondary pupils' homework and found that teachers could be highly sensitive to variations in children's home backgrounds when setting homework tasks – for example, being aware that some pupils might be unable to complete homework tasks because of the disorganization of the home.

What appears to be fundamental to the process of parental involvement influencing children's learning at school is not so much the development and honing of educational skills, such as reading or numerical competence, but rather the creation of an ethos at home that supports the child as a learner. As mentioned in Chapter 1, Desforges and Abouchaar (2003) conducted a major review of the link between parental involvement and pupil achievement. It emerged that a key feature of home support is parents modelling positive aspirations that help the child to construct a pro-learning self-concept and high educational self-expectations:

> **RESEARCH QUOTATION**
>
> *'. . . parental involvement seems to have its major impact on children* [as measured by achievement at school] *through the modelling of values and expectations . . . It seems that pupils internalise aspects of parental values and expectations as they form an image of themselves as a learner – their so-called 'educational self schema.'*
>
> **Desforges and Abouchaar, 2003, p. 51**

Russell and Granville (2005) have found that although many parents may recognize that it is important to provide the sort of learning support and educational input at home that Desforges describes, parents are often unaware of the **marked extent** to which such involvement impacts on children's achievement at school. This may not be surprising, given that it is only recently that research has begun to tease out which aspects of parental involvement play a major role in children's learning. There are strong grounds for teachers explaining to parents that the family's influence in developing positive attitudes to learning at home can have a direct and substantial impact on enhancing children's progress at school.

An important theme to emerge from research is that although certain factors tend to influence the involvement levels of all parents (e.g. the age of the child or the phase of schooling), there are striking variations **between** parental groups in their level of engagement with teachers. This raises the question as to why some parents' involvement in their child's education is low, and why some parents experience difficulties in engaging with schools. The following section addresses these issues and considers conceptualizations of parents who may be considered hard to reach.

Risk factors and 'hard to reach' parents and carers

Some parents are viewed as harder to reach than others. Doherty et al. (2004) conducted research for the National Foundation for Educational Research into professionals' perceptions of marginalized or vulnerable groups, exploring how 'hard to reach families' are defined. The professionals interviewed in this study were involved in the *On Track* programme. This is an early intervention scheme set up in areas characterized by high deprivation; it is designed to reduce and prevent crime for 'at risk' children aged 4 to 12 and their families. Interventions included home visiting, the development of home–school partnerships and parenting support and training. At an early stage, practitioners became aware that some 'hard to reach' groups were reluctant to take advantage of the provision on offer. Three main definitions of such groups were used by these professionals:

- **Minority groups.** The traditionally under-represented groups, the marginalized, disadvantaged or socially excluded; for example minority ethnic families, travellers and asylum seekers.
- **Slipping through the net.** The overlooked, the 'invisible' or individuals unable to articulate their needs. This conceptualization includes those who fall just outside the statutory or usual remit of a service provider, or those whose needs may not be sufficiently acute to warrant access to a service.
- **The service resistant.** Those unwilling to engage with service providers, the suspicious, the disaffected or over-targeted. This definition includes families (known to agencies such as social services) that are distrustful of service providers.

Doherty et al. found that very little consultation was occurring with families during services' development and planning stages, partly because engaging hard to reach groups could be costly in terms of time and resources. It was also found that when consultation did take place the same people tended to be repeatedly contacted and asked to represent all hard to reach groups. Although Doherty et al.'s study focused on out-of-school services aimed at crime prevention and reduction, nevertheless there are implications for how teachers define and liaise with hard to reach parents. In *Every Child Matters: Change for Schools* (Department for Education and Skills, 2003d) schools are encouraged to offer a range of extended services and build stronger relationships with parents and the wider community. With such developments, clarity about definitions of hard to reach parents and consultation procedures within communities will be important. Such marginalized groups might include those experiencing marked poverty, parents from certain minority ethnic groups, carers of looked-after children, parents of disabled children, and refugee and travelling families (Doherty et al., 2004; Moon and Ivins, 2004; Russell and Granville, 2005).

Families living in poverty

When 'hard to reach' groups are discussed in the research and policy literature, poverty frequently emerges as a factor that precipitates and maintains exclusion and marginalization. Although there is no standard definition of poverty, Palmer et al. (2006) suggest that a family is defined as living in poverty if its income is less than 60% of the contemporary average household income, after income tax and housing costs have been deducted. In 2004/2005, the poverty income level was set at £268 (or less) per week for a couple with two children. The amount remaining after deduction of tax and housing costs (i.e. weekly income) is what the family has to spend on everything else it needs such as food, heating, travel and entertainment.

The United Kingdom has a higher proportion of its population on relatively low income than 9 of the 15 'pre-accession' countries (countries that formed the European Union up to 2004). Furthermore, the gap between the rich and the poor remains wide: over the last decade, the incomes of the richest 10% in the United Kingdom have increased the most, whereas incomes of the poorest 10% have increased the least. In previous years, if one or both parents were in employment this was often taken as an indicator by schools and other agencies that there were probably sufficient resources to provide an acceptable standard of living for children. Today, however, this might well not be the case, for employment does not necessarily protect families from poverty. Two-fifths of children in low-income households are cared for by couples where at least one of the adults is in paid work (Palmer et al., 2006). Furthermore, research evidence indicates that work commitments can actually create a barrier to parents becoming more involved in their child's education (Williams et al., 2002). Such responsibilities impact particularly acutely on parents in low-paid occupations who work long hours where there is little flexibility to enable attendance at school-based events such as parents' evenings.

Another poverty-related barrier to parental involvement that is frequently cited in research is difficulty in securing and paying for childcare, particularly for parents with very young children (Williams et al., 2002; Moon and Ivins, 2004; Russell and Granville, 2005).

The Joseph Rowntree Foundation's *Education and Poverty* programme has established that children growing up in poverty are less likely to achieve well at school. One of the Foundation's aims is to examine the root causes of poverty and disadvantage, identify solutions, and influence government policy and practice in this field (www.jrf.org.uk). For some years the government has recognized that tackling low income is imperative – poverty is viewed as not only a cause of social exclusion but also a consequence, and that it impacts severely on children's learning and development. It appears that UK policy makers are taking account of the numerous studies that have been conducted in this field, and of the views of eminent scholars such as Peter Mittler, who has commented on the damaging and corrosive impact that poverty has on families' capacity to engage positively with their children's education. Mittler (2000) presents a forceful account of the extent to which having little money and living below the poverty line produce considerable hardship for families:

RESEARCH QUOTATION

'It [poverty] *causes immense stress and worry to parents and carers, leaving them little time to enjoy their children, far less cooperate with schools in promoting their child's learning. It has a major effect on nutrition and general health and therefore heightens vulnerability to illness and accidents. It is nearly always linked to sub-standard housing and to overcrowding, which in turn makes it difficult for children to find a quiet corner.*'

Mittler, 2000, p. 49

There are indications that UK policy makers recognize that poverty is closely linked to poor attainment, and in order to promote a fairer and more inclusive society the UK government aims to eradicate child poverty by 2020 (HM Treasury, 2005).

Parents from minority ethnic groups

Another factor that can influence parents' engagement with schools is ethnic status, and a key challenge facing schools is how to ensure that pupils from diverse social backgrounds and cultures achieve well. The school achievement of some minority ethic pupils is significantly and consistently weak, particularly the performance of pupils of Bangladeshi, Pakistani and African-Caribbean heritage. Concern about the achievement of minority ethnic groups has been voiced for a number of years in the United Kingdom. Gillborn and Mirza (2000) asserted that inequalities of attainment in GCSE examinations placed African-Caribbean, Pakistani and Bangladeshi pupils in a disadvantaged position. Five years later Carpenter and Lall (2005) raised similar concerns: 'Despite an overall improvement in standards since the late 1980s, the major inequalities of attainment remain between white pupils and their peers of Bangladeshi, Pakistani and African Caribbean heritage' (p. 4). It is worth noting, however, that in a recent review of literature conducted by Mongon and Chapman (2008) it emerged that some white children's achievement was falling behind. An analysis was made of evidence mainly from the United Kingdom, concentrating on underachievement amongst low-income student groups. The magnitude as well as persistence of underachievement amongst pupils from low-income families was acute, and apart from 'traveller' students, the group with the lowest attainment in schools was white British boys and girls entitled to free school meals (the most commonly used indicator of deprivation).

In the United Kingdom, Gill Crozier has written extensively about the involvement of black and other minority ethnic parents in education. She argues that there exists an overarching assumption amongst education professionals that all parents are the same and that their children can be treated in the same way. She is concerned that a 'one size fits all' approach to parental involvement obscures the roles that minority ethnic parents are playing, the complexity of their needs and the barriers that undermine their involvement. Crozier suggests that schools' policies for engaging families generally fail to recognize ethnic diversity amongst parents, and that this may contribute to widening the gap between the involved and the uninvolved (Crozier, 2001).

Crozier (2004) conducted a 2-year project focusing on the experiences of Bangladeshi and Pakistani families in North East England. Many of the Bangladeshi parents in this study had not been educated in the United Kingdom and most of the Bangladeshi mothers spoke very little English and knew little about the education system; for example, some parents were not aware of the assessment or setting systems used in schools. Although mothers of younger children were beginning to make more contact with schools, there was generally limited contact between Bangladeshi parents and teachers in primary and secondary schools. Where contact had been made, it tended to be initiated by the school and generally focused on disciplinary issues. Few Bangladeshi parents opted to play a direct role in their children's education. They felt that their responsibility was to provide a supportive home and family background and to give general encouragement to their children. In contrast, Pakistani parents' knowledge and understanding of school systems was more developed. Although they were generally satisfied with their children's experience of primary school, they were more critical of secondary schools, and a particular concern voiced by many Pakistani parents was that secondary teachers tended to have low expectations regarding their children's achievement. Crozier found that secondary teachers' contact with parents tended to be impersonal and written communication was the dominant method. Many of the Bangladeshi parents and some Pakistani parents were not able to read the information sent home by schools. Extended families played an important part in children's education, but this tended not to receive the same level of acknowledgement from the teachers as that of the parents' involvement. Head teachers confirmed that Bangladeshi parents' contact with school was limited, and Crozier comments that a lack of visibility seemed to result in the assumption of head teachers that Bangladeshi parents were not generally interested in their children's education.

Some minority ethnic parents have taken radical steps to address perceived inequalities in the education system. Reay and Mirza (2005) present an account of African-Caribbean groups who set up four supplementary schools (three in London, one in another city), run after school and on Saturdays or Sundays. Parents (mainly mothers) attributed their decision to provide supplementary education for their children to concerns about the racism both they and their children experienced in schools, and to perceptions of teachers' low expectations. Reay and Mirza explain that supplementary schools are mainly run by women and have a history that dates back to the 1950s when the first groups of post-war immigrants settled in Britain. These authors located 60 black supplementary schools in the London area:

RESEARCH QUOTATION

'. . . the schools are difficult to locate as they exist deep within the black community and are hidden away from the public gaze of funders and local authorities. They go quietly about their business in community centres, church halls, empty classrooms, and even the front rooms of dedicated black educators.'

Reay and Mirza, 2005, p. 137

An unexpected finding in Reay and Mirza's research was that the choice of curriculum created tensions between the black educators running these supplementary schools and the parents of the children who attended them. Mothers voiced their desire for an emphasis on 'the basics' (English and Mathematics), whereas the black educators wished to promote a broader curriculum that included more creative elements (e.g. dance and drama), black history and black studies.

Indications that positive relations between schools and African-Caribbean parents can be difficult to achieve come from the evaluation of the *Aiming High* project, a government initiative to raise the achievement of African-Caribbean pupils in 30 secondary schools (Tikly et al., 2006). Many schools identified parental involvement as the most difficult area to tackle. When exploring families' perspectives, it was noted that the schooling of black people in Britain left a negative legacy for some African-Caribbean parents who had experienced racist attitudes. Another finding to emerge from the *Aiming High* project was parents' apprehension about inconsistent and poor communication with schools – parents were concerned about the delay in receiving information about important academic or behaviour issues at school. Some schools in the project, however, had developed a range of strategies for effective communication, using phone calls, e-mails and texting as well as pupil diaries to facilitate rapid exchanges of information between teachers and parents.

In another study that examined the views of parents and carers of black African, black Caribbean, Pakistani, Bangladeshi and mixed heritage groups, Moon and Ivins (2004) asked parents about their confidence in helping their child with homework. About one-third of parents of children from Pakistani and Bangladeshi backgrounds expressed a lack of assurance in this area, as did parents for whom English was not their first language. The main reason given by parents for their lack of confidence was difficulty in understanding the work set for their child. When parents from minority ethnic groups who described themselves as 'not very involved' with school were asked how they would like to be more involved, they mentioned that they would like more opportunities to talk to teachers, help out in the classroom and contribute generally to school events.

Carers of looked-after children

Another group who may be viewed as hard to engage are carers of looked-after children. The government report *Care Matters* (Department for Education and Skills, 2006) refers to the 'shocking statistics' on the poor quality of education of children in care, which, it is anticipated, will have devastating long-term outcomes for children: only 11% of children in care attained five good GCSEs in 2005, compared with 56% of all children; similar attainment gaps exist for these children throughout all phases of education. An earlier report (Department of Education and Skills, 2003a) on children in care presents some stark outcomes (Box 2.2).

Box 2.2   Statistics on looked-after children in England (taken from Department for Education and Skills, 2003a).

- At any one time, around 60 000 children are being looked after.
- Only 1% of looked-after children go on to attend university (compared with 40–45% of all school leavers).
- Approximately 25% of looked-after children have a statement of special educational needs (compared with around 3% of all children).
- Approximately 25% of children in care are placed outside their 'home' Local Authority.
- Contrary to commonly held beliefs, the great majority of children (80%) enter care not because of their own behaviour but because of abuse, neglect or other family reasons.
- Around 66% of looked-after children live in foster care; only 10% are placed in children's homes.

As mentioned above, levels of achievement of looked-after children are extremely low, and some research has focused on the relationship between those responsible for looked-after children (social workers, foster parents and other carers) and schools. For most children, natural parents provide levels of encouragement and support that are carefully judged, robust and consistent. A key aspect of such support is its steadfastness – children know that at times of uncertainty or need they could generally depend on an adult who has known them intimately over the period of their lifetime, and who is prepared to act as an advocate on their behalf. This may not be the case with looked-after children, who tend to lack a consistent adult in their lives. Therefore, the Department for Education and Skills (2006) emphasizes the importance of teachers recognizing that social workers may have only limited autonomy to act as strong, vocal advocates for children in care.

There are a number of reasons why social workers experience difficulties in being effective advocates for children and young people. Children's social workers take on a corporate parenting role, but high turnover rates substantially undermine their ability to act as a consistent parent. The Department for Education and Skills (2006) reports that over half the Local Authorities who participated in a survey of provision for looked-after children reported problems with the recruitment and retention of children's social workers. This can occur because of social workers' frustration with complex systems that undermine direct work with children and young people. Harker (2004) suggests that another barrier that can undermine effective liaison between social workers and teachers is the existence of conflicting priorities. Heavy workloads can prevent social workers from seeing education as a priority, compared with urgent placement issues and concerns about children and young people's emotional or physical needs. Conversely, current pressures on teachers such as the pervasive emphasis on raising standards may not be conducive to investing time in contacting and liaising with social workers about looked-after children. In the government's White Paper *Care Matters: Time for Change* (Department for Education and Skills, 2007a), a number of steps are set out for improving outcomes for children and young people in care, including a proposal that schools appoint a 'designated teacher' for looked-after children. Such a teacher's responsibilities would cover not only schooling issues (such as ensuring that appropriate teaching and learning is put in place) but also liaison with children's carers in order to promote good home–school links. In *Care Matters: Time to Deliver for Children in Care* (Department for Education and Skills, 2008), there is a welcome announcement that the role of designated teachers will become statutory.

One of the most concerning issues in the interface between schools and carers of looked-after children is the lack of availability of detailed information. Jacklin et al. (2006) report that despite higher than ever numbers of children being placed in care, there are indications in the United Kingdom that reliable records are not maintained. In a study exploring the challenge of raising the attainment of children in care, it emerged that Local Authority agencies were unable to identify clearly the children for whom they were responsible. The authors report that approximately one-third of Year 11 students identified as looked-after by education officials in a specified area in one Local Authority did not appear to be known to social services; and in terms of school/carer communication, in many cases it was not possible to establish the identity of the receiving person when schools sent a letter 'home'. These researchers conclude that there has been a limited awareness of education within the care system, and conversely a limited awareness of care within the education system.

Parents of children with special educational needs and disabled children

Much of the research on parental involvement and children with special educational needs focuses on parents' relationships with professionals responsible for diagnosing and assessing young children, such as doctors and psychologists. Less has been written about the relationships between parents (of school-age children) with special needs and teachers. However, it is increasingly acknowledged that this group of parents may experience considerable difficulties engaging with teachers and other professionals. The Audit Commission report *Special Educational Needs: A Mainstream Issue* (Audit Commission, 2002) asked parent-partnership officers which parents they considered were 'hard to reach'. Parents of children with special educational needs from minority ethnic groups and those who did not speak English as a first language were highlighted by almost two-thirds of respondents. The UK government's *Special Educational Needs Code of Practice* (Department for Education and Skills, 2001) forcefully emphasizes why parents play such a crucial part in supporting children with special needs, and why professionals (including teachers) need to work actively with parents and need to seek out and value their input: 'Parents hold key information and have a critical role to play in their children's education. They have unique strengths, knowledge and experience to contribute to the shared view of a child's needs and the best ways of supporting them' (Department for Education and Skills, 2001, Section 2, p. 2).

The *Special Educational Needs Code of Practice* recommends that schools carry out regular reviews of their policies to ensure that they encourage active partnership with parents and avoid creating barriers to participation. Key principles for schools are set out when communicating and working in partnership with parents, which include the following:

- Providing user-friendly information and developing procedures that are easy to understand.
- Avoiding presumptions about what parents can or cannot do to support their children's learning.
- Bearing in mind the pressures a parent may be under because of their child's needs.

Poverty is a significant factor that may affect families with a child with special needs and their capacity to form cooperative links with schools. Buchanan et al. (2004) note that parents with disabled children are at particular risk of poverty and social exclusion because they generally have lower incomes. Parents of disabled children are much less likely to be in full-time employment compared with parents of non-disabled children, and although disability benefits can contribute to families' income, these are often insufficient as it costs up to three times as much to bring up a severely disabled child as a non-disabled child. Furthermore, appropriate childcare for disabled children tends to be more expensive and can be difficult to locate. So this too is likely to impact on parents' ability to make arrangements for attending school-based events and liaise with teachers.

Apart from a lack of financial resources, a range of other factors can act against the development of good communication between parents of children with special needs and teachers. The House of Commons Committee (2006) reports that the sheer complexity of policies and procedures and the rate at which these change make it difficult for both teachers and parents to understand such frameworks and how these are interpreted locally. This will undoubtedly affect communication between schools and parents. Furthermore, some children with special needs are bussed or taxied to mainstream schools and this can impair home–school links; so too can the need for some children to make frequent visits to hospital to see specialists.

Beveridge (2005) comments that most parents at some stage need to speak out on behalf of their children, but the need for advocacy is intensified for parents of children with special needs. This is partly due to the fact that parents may need to question and challenge the level and type of provision offered by Local Authorities, particularly when mainstream placements are sought. The government report *Removing Barriers to Achievement* (Department for Education and Skills, 2004e) refers to a culture of mistrust that can build up between parents and professionals, resulting in parents feeling the need to 'fight' for the support to which their child is entitled. Clearly, such pressures may undermine the development of trusting relationships between schools and families and may contribute to some parents being viewed as harder to reach.

Some parents are more effective than others at engaging with schools and Local Authorities when adopting an advocating role on behalf of their children. The Audit Commission (2002) noted that parents of children with special needs without the knowledge, resources and confidence to question staff in schools and Local Authorities are less likely to get their child's needs assessed and to secure a generous package of provision. It cannot be overemphasized how stressful it can be for parents to bring up children with chronic and high levels of needs, including children with severe learning and communication difficulties and children on the autistic spectrum. International research involving families coping with children with different types of disabilities demonstrates significant levels of emotional strain, high rates of marital breakdown, and mental health problems and depression amongst parents (Dyson, 1993; Wallander and Varni, 1998). For such parents, some of the most distressing factors relate to the management of problem behaviour (Besag, 2002; Saloviita et al., 2003). Faced with such pressures, it is understandable why some families with children with special needs may not have sufficient time or energy to maintain consistent links with schools.

Asylum seekers and refugees

The UK government's report *Aiming High: Guidance on Supporting the Education of Asylum Seeking and Refugee Children* (Department for Education and Skills, 2004a) defines asylum seekers as those who leave their home country and search for refugee status in another, and then apply for asylum with that government. Unlike most immigrants, refugees do not leave their homes by choice – they are generally forced out of their home countries, often in violent circumstances such as civil war (McBrien, 2005). Families are recognized as refugees once the government accepts that the families meet the formal United Nations definition and decides that the families have a well-founded fear of being persecuted. In the United Kingdom, children who are asylum seekers or refugees are entitled to education up to the age of 16.

Although asylum-seeking and refugee families can experience marked difficulties when arriving in the United Kingdom and parents may be perceived as hard to reach, a number of positive experiences and features have been documented, and it is worth reviewing these before exploring the challenges in this field. The Office for Standards in Education (2003) has noted that many schools receiving asylum-seeking and refugee children are enterprising in finding interpreters from the local community and go to great lengths to ensure that parents are an integral part of the welcome and induction: '[Such schools] gave careful attention to informing the parents not just about the education of their children and their entitlements, such as free school meals, but also about facilities in the local community' (Office for Standards in Education, 2003, p. 11). One school in the Midlands arranged a series of acclimatizing events and activities for asylum-seeking and refugee parents, including family literacy groups and adult English classes. Another school appointed a bilingual assistant who spoke the language of the newly arrived families to ensure that there was effective communication between staff, children and parents.

The literature on asylum-seeking and refugee parents does not focus exclusively on benefits that flow from schools to families – there are encouraging reports of benefits that operate in the opposite direction, from asylum-seeking and refugee families to schools. Reakes and Powell (2004) report that asylum-seeking children can contribute an increased cultural richness and diversity to the school as a whole; and the Office for Standards in Education (2003) reports that many asylum-seeking pupils make good progress in relatively short periods of time, partly because of strong support from their parents.

A theme in the literature on asylum-seeking and refugee families that echoes Crozier's concern about the prevalence of typecast attitudes towards minority ethnic parents is the danger that such families are perceived and responded to as if they are a homogeneous group, with similar requirements and needs. Milbourne (2002) conducted research in two deprived inner-city areas in the United Kingdom, drawing on the experiences of non-English-speaking women and children and other culturally excluded groups, including asylum seekers and refugees of Bengali, Somali, Turkish, Afghan and Kosovan origin. She stresses that hard to reach groups are not identical: families come from diverse communities and cultures and may speak a wide range of languages, and their expectations and experience of education may differ considerably. A similar finding emerged from a study of asylum seekers in Wales (Reakes and Powell, 2004) in which a specialist teacher emphasized that asylum seekers' individual needs should be recognized:

RESEARCH QUOTATION

'People think that asylum seekers are a homogenous group, but they come from different backgrounds, different countries ... We've got so many different nationalities and therefore different cultures and religions, different experiences and different educational experiences.'

Reakes and Powell, 2004, p. 22

The challenges that confront asylum-seeking and refugee families when they first arrive in a new country are typically immense. According to Russell and Granville (2005), asylum seekers and refugees often lack essential information about how local services and schools operate and may not know where to go to access this information. This can result in extreme social exclusion and isolation, which in turn can make it difficult for schools to liaise with parents. Russell and Granville comment that asylum seekers and refugees are often housed in estates where levels of social deprivation are high, and where schools may experience considerable challenges in generating a strong sense of community. In such conditions, it is understandable why such families may not engage consistently with school activities.

Currently, the great majority of asylum-seeking and refugee children come from homes where little or no English is spoken – over 70%, according the government (Department for Education and Skills, 2004a) – and schools may well be the setting where they first experience the English language. Difficulty with interpretation can become a major barrier to effective communication between schools and families, and this is mentioned by numerous commentators. Milbourne (2002) has found that parents, particularly women, depend markedly on local community groups, which themselves are often vulnerable because of poor levels of resourcing and support, placing an enormous strain on a small number of individuals.

Once asylum-seeking or refugee children have found a school, they often adapt to their new context swiftly. However, this adjustment can mask difficulties at home. McBrien (2005) notes that refugee children can overtake their parents when learning English and they may be called on to take on adult roles and translate when their parents meet professionals such as doctors and teachers. McBrien warns that 'cultural dissonance' may develop when parents begin to lag behind their children in developing the language and culture of their new country, which can result in tense, intergenerational family conflicts.

Parents of travelling children

The generic term 'traveller' has been used to describe groups whose way of life is nomadic or semi-nomadic. In the United Kingdom, these might include Gypsies/Romanies of English, Scottish or Welsh heritage, Gypsies and travellers of Irish heritage, Roma/Gypsies mainly from Eastern and Central Europe, Fairground Families, New Age travellers, Circus Families, Bargees and other families living on boats (Bhopal, 2004; Department for Education and Skills, 2005a). However, the term traveller can be problematic and confusing. The Commission for Racial Equality (www.cre.gov.uk) points out that although some groups are highly itinerant and may move from one place to another according to the availability of work opportunities, others may travel only for limited periods, returning to their home base for the winter months. Furthermore, although the majority of Gypsies and Irish travellers live in caravans on Local Authority or privately owned sites (with a minority living on the roadside or in unauthorized encampments because of the scarcity of legal sites) many Gypsies and Irish travellers have opted to reside **permanently** in privately owned houses or in council housing.

The term Gypsy traveller is currently preferred by a number of authors. Official figures for the overall number of Gypsy travellers in the United Kingdom are not currently available. However, according to the Gypsy and traveller web site *Friends, Gypsies and Travellers* (www.gypsy-traveller.org), in 2003 there were approximately 4000 Irish traveller pupils and 6000 Gypsy/Roma pupils registered in schools. It is known that Gypsy and Irish traveller children, particularly those of secondary age, have much lower levels of school attendance than pupils from other groups. By Key Stage 3, it is estimated that only 15–20% of traveller pupils are registered or regularly attend school (Commission for Racial Equality; www.cre.gov.uk).

There are various reasons why Gypsy traveller parents may experience difficulties engaging with schools and why they may be viewed as harder to reach by teachers. Family ties and shared aspirations are strongly featured in the literature on Gypsy traveller communities, and parents may have forebodings about the impact of schooling on their children's values and beliefs. At a general level, although many parents hold positive views about education, a topic that permeates the literature focuses on parents' misgivings about whether it is possible to achieve integration in mainstream education whilst preserving the values and cultural identity for Gypsy traveller groups (Hately-Broad, 2004; Bhopal, 2004). A number of more specific factors have been identified that can contribute to a lack of contact between Gypsy traveller parents and schools:

- Families may work seasonally or may experience unpredictable, forced eviction, which can result in interrupted educational experiences. Temporary accommodation and moving frequently create considerable challenges for families, especially women. Such factors undermine community and family support networks and can result in parents feeling excluded and alienated from their children's schooling (Department for Education and Skills, 2003a; Milbourne, 2002).

- Many Gypsy traveller parents have very limited experience of education, and may not have attended secondary school. Therefore, they may be markedly unconfident about entering schools and approaching and talking with teachers. Derrington and Kendall (2004) found that only one in three Gypsy traveller parents said that they had attended parents' evenings in primary school, and this proportion fell to one in four for children in secondary schools. The principal reason for non-attendance at these meetings was parents' lack of confidence.

- In *Aiming High: Raising the Achievement of Gypsy Traveller Pupils. A Guide to Good Practice* (Department for Education and Skills, 2003b), it is noted that many Gypsy traveller parents have few literacy skills, making it difficult for them to know how best to support their children.

- A number of studies have reported that a key concern of Gypsy traveller parents is the high level of racist name-calling and bullying within schools and the community, and that this may not be acknowledged by teachers (Lloyd and Stead, 2001). However, in a study conducted by Jordan (2001) traveller parents emphasized that in their view it was not school staff that were to blame but the other children and the local community – they viewed schools as less blatantly racist than society in general.

Bhopal has conducted extensive research exploring Gypsy traveller groups' perspectives on identity and education (Bhopal and Myers, 2008). She notes that the 1994 Criminal Justice and Public Order Act removed the obligation on Local Authorities to provide official sites for these families. Such sites have become scarcer and many families have been forced to reside in illegal roadside encampments. As a result many Gypsy travellers move constantly to avoid eviction, and this in turn results in irregular school attendance and has a detrimental effect on children's education. However, Bhopal strongly challenges the customary notion that Gypsy traveller parents are not interested in sending their children to school. In an in-depth study that involved 20 families, Bhopal (2004) found that parents' attitudes to education appeared to be increasingly supportive. Many of the parents in this study commented on the restrictions on Gypsy travellers' traditional lifestyles. Much of the work traditionally related to the Gypsy traveller lifestyle was diminishing and parents anticipated that it might not exist in future. Parents predicted that their children would probably not continue in the family line of business and this prompted them to reconsider the changing prospects for their children earning a living. Therefore, there was a mounting tendency to view education as a stepping stone into non-traditional Gypsy traveller occupations. It is worth noting that many of the parents interviewed were very positive about the quality of support they received from the Traveller Education Service (TES). However, Bhopal comments that although the TES is valued, schools still need to develop strong links with the Gypsy traveller community and not over-depend on TES personnel to assume responsibility for such work.

Conclusions

The factors that impinge on parents' capacity to engage with schools are complex and diverse and include poverty and social deprivation, ethnicity and the experience of disability. Some groups experience persistent, unrelenting levels of disadvantage that can be difficult to avoid. However, terms that are used to describe those experiencing such problems need to be used judiciously. Labels such as 'the under-class' or 'the hard to reach' are socially constructed and do not provide explanations about why certain groups experience difficulties. In the following chapters, projects are discussed that have been successful in engaging parents who might experience difficulties engaging with schools. We start with an examination of initiatives from international perspectives.

3

International Perspectives

Introduction

Collaboration between education professionals and families is attracting increasing attention internationally. This chapter considers developments that have impacted on practice in countries other than the United Kingdom. In the United States, research on parental involvement in education is characterized by a strong emphasis on approaches for involving parents who experience difficulties in becoming engaged with schools. The US-based Southwest Educational Development Laboratory has published a series of syntheses of studies conducted in the United States on school, family and community connections; these publications present a rich and detailed overview of investigations into this field. In her research synthesis *Diversity: School, Family and Community Connections*, Boethel (2003) reviews projects that target the involvement of minority and low-income families. One of the findings is that interventions tend to focus more on changing parents' behaviour than changing school practices. This is a topic that strongly resonates with the core theme of this book, that is, there is much scope for schools to explore how provision can be

Engaging 'Hard to Reach' Parents: Teacher–Parent Collaboration to Promote Children's Learning By Anthony Feiler © 2010 John Wiley & Sons, Ltd

adapted to meet the needs of families, rather than concentrating on how parents should change to fit the school. Boethel reviewed over 60 studies and the following recommendations are included for schools and professionals aiming to help families and strengthen academic achievement amongst minority and low-income students:

- Provide families with training and resources to support early literacy.
- Help families to use specific communication and monitoring strategies to support their children's learning.
- Encourage and support student involvement in a range of school- and community-sponsored extracurricular and after-school activities.
- Help low-income families obtain the support and services they need to keep themselves safe, healthy and well fed.

An influential and frequently cited model of parental involvement has been devised by the US scholar Joyce Epstein; this chapter starts with an outline of her framework. This is followed by a discussion of the perspectives of two influential commentators who are highly respected internationally for their views on the experiences of minority students and on childhood development: Jim Cummins and Barbara Rogoff. Later in the chapter, four projects are presented and discussed: two studies from the United States (the CoZi model and an investigation of mathematics learning at home); a project from New Zealand that explored parents' involvement in assessment; and an account of Reggio Emilia children's centres in Italy, where there is a strong focus on family involvement. The principal rationale for selecting these initiatives is that they represent imaginative responses to the challenge of involving parents who might experience difficulties in engaging with teachers and other professionals. These four international projects include examples of good practice that staff in other schools and settings might adapt in order to suit local circumstances.

First, Joyce Epstein's model of parental involvement is considered – a framework that explores actions that schools might consider when developing home–school partnerships.

Joyce Epstein's model of parental involvement

Joyce Epstein (2001) presents six areas within the field of parenting and home–school links where there exist key opportunities for schools to collaborate closely with parents to help children's and young people's development (Box 3.1).

Box 3.1   Joyce Epstein's six types of parental involvement (taken from Epstein, 2001, pp. 409–411).

1. Parenting
Help all families establish home environments to support children as students, for example workshops, videotapes, computerized phone messages on parenting and child rearing at each age and grade level; parent education and other courses or training for parents. 'Workshop' refers to more than a meeting about a topic held at school – it may include making information about a topic available in a variety of forms that can be viewed, heard or read.

Challenges
- Provide information to **all** families who want it or who need it, not just to the few who can attend workshops or meetings at the school building.
- Enable families to share information with schools about culture, background, children's talents and needs.
- Make sure that all information for and from families is clear, usable and linked to children's success in school.

2. Communicating
Design effective forms for school-to-home and home-to-school communications about school programmes and children's progress (two-way, three-way and many-way channels of communication that connect schools, families, students and the community), for example conferences with every parent at least

(continued)

---

once a year, with follow-ups as needed; language translators to assist families as needed.

Challenges

- Review the readability, clarity, form and frequency of all memos, notices and other print and non-print communications.
- Consider parents who do not speak English well, do not read well or need large font type.
- Review the quality of major communications (e.g. newsletters, report cards and conference schedules).
- Establish clear two-way channels for communications from home to school and from school to home.

3. Volunteering

Recruit and organize parent help and support (or any adult who supports school goals and children's learning or development in any way, at any place and at any time, not just during the school day and at the school building), for example a parent room or family centre for volunteer work, meetings, resources for families; annual postcard survey to identify all available talents, availability and locations of volunteers.

Challenges

- Recruit volunteers widely so that all families know that their time and talents are welcome.
- Make flexible schedules for volunteers, assemblies and events to enable the participation of parents who work at odd hours.
- Organize volunteer work; provide training; match time and talent with school, teacher, and student needs; and recognize efforts so that participants become more productive.

4. Learning at home

Provide information and ideas to families about how to help students at home with homework and other curriculum-related activities, decisions and planning, for example information for families on skills required for students in all subjects at each grade; family mathematics, science, and reading activities at school.

'Homework' refers not only to work done alone but also interactive activities shared with others at home or in the community, linking schoolwork to real life.

Challenges
- Design and organize a regular schedule of interactive homework (e.g. weekly or bimonthly) that gives students responsibility for discussing important things they are learning and helps families stay aware of the content of their children's classwork.
- Coordinate family-linked homework activities, if students have several teachers.
- Involve families and their children in all-important curriculum-related decisions.

5. Decision-making
Include parents in school decisions, developing parent leaders and representatives, for example active PTA or other parent organizations, advisory councils or committees; networks to link all families with parent representatives. 'Decision-making' means a process of partnership, of shared views and actions towards shared goals, not just a power struggle between conflicting ideas.

Challenges
- Include parent leaders from all racial, ethnic, socioeconomic and other groups in the school.
- Offer training to enable leaders to serve as representatives of other families, with input from and return of information to all parents.
- Include students (along with parents) in decision-making groups.

6. Collaborating with community
Identify and integrate resources and services from the community to strengthen school programmes, family practices and student learning and development, for example information for students and families on community health, cultural, recreational, social

(*continued*)

support and other programmes or services; service integration through partnerships involving school, civic, health, recreation and other agencies and organizations; and businesses. 'Community' refers not only to the neighbourhoods where students' homes and schools are located but also any neighbourhoods that influence their learning and development. 'Community' also means all who are interested in and affected by the quality of education, not just those with children in the schools.

Challenges
- Solve turf problems of responsibilities, funds, staff and locations for collaborative activities.
- Inform families of community programmes for students, such as mentoring, tutoring, business partnerships.
- Assure equity of opportunities for students and families to participate in community programmes or to obtain services.
- Match community contributions with school goals and integrate child and family services with education.

Some commentators have suggested that Epstein's framework is rather school dominated and tends to play down how parents are already supporting their children in ways that might be overlooked by teachers (Jackson and Remillard, 2005). Nevertheless, a strongly inclusive theme underpins the challenges that Epstein identifies – challenges that explicitly address the issue of schools taking account of the barriers that face some parents who might be 'harder to reach'. This is the topic explored by Jim Cummins, who examines why students from certain 'minority' backgrounds and cultures tend to perform poorly at school.

Viewpoints from Jim Cummins: teachers' potential for empowering minority students by reaching out to communities

Jim Cummins works at the University of Toronto in Canada and his research encompasses language and literacy development of learners of English as an additional language. In 1986 Cummins wrote a landmark article 'Empowering minority students: a framework for intervention' in which he explored the educational and social barriers that undermine academic achievement for culturally diverse pupils. A framework was presented for analysing the international trend for minority students to fail at school. In using the term 'minority students', Cummins refers to two broad groups: students whose home language and culture differ from those of the school and wider society (language minority students), and students whose first language may be English, but whose cultural background differs significantly from that of the school and of wider society (culturally diverse students). In Britain, such groups might comprise pupils of Bangladeshi, Pakistani and African-Caribbean heritage, whose progress at school has raised concerns for some years (as mentioned in Chapter 2). Cummins seeks to identify reasons why minority students from such dominated groups tend to perform poorly at school. He argues that this occurs predominantly because of inequalities in status and power relations that are endemic in **societies**, and that these inequalities tend to be reflected in schools. A compelling example is presented: at the time Cummins was writing, Finnish students in Sweden were perceived as having a relatively low social status and their academic achievement at school was weak; whereas in Australia, during the same period, Finnish students' social status was high and they accordingly achieved academic success at school.

An important proposition made by Cummins is that schools are very well positioned to counteract the negative, discriminatory influence of society: minority students can be empowered as a direct result of their interactions with teachers. This hinges not only on how teachers relate to such students, but also on the extent to which minority family and community participation is encouraged by schools as a fundamental component of children's education. Cummins argues robustly that one of the key factors affecting minority students' progress at school is the quality of relationships that have developed between the school and the minority community. He strongly feels that the great majority of parents want to help their children learn, but may lack the skills or confidence to become involved. It is proposed that where sound, respectful relations are established between teachers and parents of minority ethnic pupils and with the wider minority community, parents' sense of self-efficacy will increase and will be communicated to children, and this in turn will impact positively on their attainment:

RESEARCH QUOTATION

'...most parents of minority students have high aspirations for their children ... However, they often do not know how to help their children academically ... Dramatic changes in children's academic progress can be realized when educators take the initiative to change this exclusionary pattern to one of collaboration.'

Cummins, 1986, p. 23

Fifteen years after the publication of this ground-breaking article, Cummins (2001) reflected on developments in the field of minority ethnic students' achievement at school. He notes that in the United States the ensuing emphasis on raising standards has forced schools and teachers to become more accountable: curriculum standards are specified and tested in order to monitor students' and schools' performance, and schools and teachers who fail are identified. Cummins argues that far from strengthening the educational system, such reforms may produce the opposite effect. The position taken in his earlier publication was reaffirmed – that power structures in society tend to re-occur in schools, and that a core reason why minority ethnic students continue to fail academically is the persisting social and educational inequalities that devalue their identity in society as well as in schools.

The positive side to Cummins' argument (both in 1986 and 2001) is that the potential for teachers to influence minority ethnic students' performance at school is **considerable**. A strong implication is that by developing respectful connections with minority families and communities, schools can moderate the negative impact of the inequalities widely present in society. Rather than focusing on students' presumed deficits, Cummins suggests that teachers can empower students by celebrating the cultural, linguistic, imaginative and intellectual resources that children bring with them to school – resources that stem from the funds of knowledge that are available in children's families and communities.

Viewpoints from Barbara Rogoff

Barbara Rogoff is a US scholar with considerable experience in conducting research with diverse communities. Much of her research chimes with Vygotskian approaches to child development and with sociocultural viewpoints. A core aspect of sociocultural theory proposes that developments in learning are often characterized by an interaction between an expert and a novice, that is, children's learning develops when they have access to and interact with more competent others. Another interpretation of this aspect of Vygotsky's work is that when groups come together and work conjointly, a collaborative form of expertise emerges (Lantoff, 2000). Rogoff is particularly interested in researching cultural features of collaborative learning and exploring the roles of adults as guides or as instructors. She is sensitive to the need for professionals to understand others' ways of bringing up children and to avoid making value judgements about other cultures' parenting practices.

In her book *The Cultural Nature of Human Development* (2003) Rogoff discusses the challenges faced by professionals when working with people from diverse backgrounds and the dangers of assuming that our own cultural practices are in some way 'right' and are superior to those of others. Rogoff considers how professionals can avoid making assumptions that are narrowly based on their own experiences, so that understanding of human development is expanded to include other cultural approaches. Many aspects of Rogoff's commentary are of direct relevance to the work of teachers and other practitioners interacting with parents from diverse cultures. This is particularly the case in Rogoff's discussion on the need for suspending judgement, together with the importance of understanding that what may be valued in one's own culture may not necessarily be accorded the same value by others.

Moving beyond initial assumptions – suspending judgement

Rogoff proposes that the problem with many of the assumptions we make about other people is that we are not aware we are making them. An 'assumption' is, after all, often a best guess, and we may not always be mindful of the extent to which our beliefs are based on conjecture and inference. Our assumptions about other people may well be influenced by a tendency to take it for granted that how we lead our lives – for example our parenting practices and how we bring up children – is the 'best' or 'right' way. Rogoff emphasizes the importance of not jumping to conclusions about other people's life styles and how imperative it is to hold back from forming judgements until we understand how others' practices fit in with their community's way of life:

RESEARCH QUOTATION

'To impose a value judgement from one's own community on the cultural practices of another – without understanding how those practices make sense in that community – is ethnocentric.'

Rogoff, 2003, p. 15

The theme of suspending judgement links closely to another topic raised by Rogoff – the importance of understanding that parental hopes and aspirations for children's development can vary extensively and are influenced substantially by cultural outlooks.

Recognizing that the goals of development vary considerably across cultural traditions

Rogoff argues that what white, middle-class parents tend to want for themselves and for their children may not correspond closely to the goals and aspirations of other groups. It is suggested that one of the problems in this field is that many of the so-called grand theories of human development (e.g. the developmental theories of Jean Piaget) assume that human development advances in relatively predictable stages towards an agreed, desirable endpoint of maturity. This is linked to the belief that some societies can be typified as 'primitive' and should be helped to become 'advanced' like those of Western 'developed' countries. Rogoff emphasizes that judgements about the goals of human development – that is, what we see as desirable for humans to aspire to and what is viewed as the height of cultural and intellectual attainment – vary enormously across different communities. She suggests that the dangers of developing an ethnocentric standpoint can be reduced by becoming aware of the extent to which families from differing cultural traditions adopt differing aspirations.

Clearly, the issues raised by Rogoff are highly significant when education professionals work with so-called hard to reach families; for it is within the realms of such work that teachers may encounter family practices that are substantially different to their own experiences and that may be at variance with the culture and values that are dominant within the school. Remembering to 'suspend judgement' about parenting practices until this is informed by direct contact and experience is wise advice. It chimes with research related to the formation of teachers' attitudes and the finding that those who have had direct, professional experience working with children with special educational needs tend to hold more positive attitudes to inclusive education (Avramidis and Norwich, 2003).

In the rest of this chapter, four initiatives are presented that illuminate the challenging process of involving harder to reach parents in education.

Community schools and the CoZi model – the United States

Since the 1980s there has been a substantial increase in the development of 'community schools' in the United States. The model of US schools focusing on involving families in order to serve community needs pre-dates the current emphasis in UK policy (Department for Education and Skills, 2004c) on schools becoming extended. Hiatt-Michael (2003) comments that the movement for teachers to connect with the local community started in schools located in urban, disadvantaged areas, and is now gathering momentum in some parts of the United States. According to one definition 'community schools' are those that are formally connected to one or more outside organizations or agencies (e.g. the health service) or to a local business, or are schools that provide a link between the school's children/families and services from the local community, as indicated by Blank (2003):

RESEARCH QUOTATION

'[A community school] *operating in a public school building, is open to students, families, and the community before, during, and after school . . . It very often operates through a partnership between the school system and an anchor institution (e.g. a community-based organisation, child and family service agency, community development group).*'

Blank, 2003, pp. 17–18, quoted in Hiatt-Michael, 2003, p. 45

The following is an example of what a visitor to a community school might expect to find:

RESEARCH QUOTATION

'*In the entry hall adults seek legal advice for permanent residency from advanced law students attending a local university. Down the hall, employees from a local business assist students with math, or a local dental hygienist provides a demonstration on dental care. In the library, parents are practising learning a second language. In the gym, other parents are joining with their offspring in aerobics instruction. Fathers offer coaching skills in sports.*'

Hiatt-Michael, 2003, p. 46

Sheldon and Voorhis (2004) examined over 300 initiatives in the United States for developing partnerships between schools, families and communities. They comment that schools that rated their partnership with parents higher in quality tended to have more parents on school decision-making committees and tended to provide greater opportunities for what the authors termed parent–child interactive homework (where students were encouraged to share their work with family members at home). However, they note that despite schools' growing expectation that parents and local communities need to provide enriching learning environments, most teachers still leave it to families to work out **how** to be most effectively involved.

So, what constitutes an effective approach to the development of community schools? Desimone et al. (2000) evaluated a community schooling strategy called 'CoZi'. The CoZi model aims to address the needs of communities through a dual process: first, creating practices within school to ensure that parents are fully involved in collaborative decision-making processes – this approach incorporates ideas from James Comer's *School Development Program* (Comer, 1980); second, offering a range of additional childcare and other services for families and children, on the basis of the work of Edward Zigler (1989) (hence CoZi). Desimone et al. describe the main features of CoZi as follows:

- Parent and teacher participation in school-based decision-making that is underpinned by child development principles.
- Parent outreach and education, beginning at the birth of the child.
- Before- and after-school care for primary-aged children.
- Parent involvement programmes (e.g. home visiting initiatives for parents of children aged 0 to 3 years).

Desimone et al. explain that the CoZi model was piloted at an elementary school serving a predominantly low-income, African American community. For evaluation purposes, a school in the same area with a similar intake of pupils acted as a control group. The CoZi school was large in comparison with most UK primary schools: 53 teachers were on the staff, with 680 pupils (nursery to 11 years). Approximately 98% of the pupils were African American, and 60% were from mother-only families. The following practices and services were available at the CoZi school:

- **Participation in school governance.** Decision-making at the school was participatory in nature and parents were viewed as playing an integral role in this process.
- **An open door policy.** Parents were encouraged to visit the school or classrooms whenever they wished.
- **Appointment of parent educators.** Three full-time parent educators worked in the school. Their role included making links between parents and health and social services and visiting all parents before children started at school.
- **Before- and after-school care.** This was available from Mondays to Fridays, from 6.00 a.m. to 6.00 p.m., for all children.

- **Nursery provision.** There were five all-day nursery classes at the school, with a comparatively generous teacher/pupil ratio (approximately 15 children in each class).

The level of parental engagement at the CoZi school was higher than at the comparison school: parents consistently reported more frequent involvement in events such as school-based adult clubs, school workshops, fund-raising meetings and a range of classroom level activities. Results from questionnaire and interview findings indicated that this might have occurred because of the proactive parental initiatives developed by the parent educators at the CoZi school, and because of shared decision-making. Importantly, higher rates of parental involvement might also have been prompted by differences in teachers' attitude and practice in the two schools. It emerged that CoZi teachers not only adopted a more supportive outlook towards family participation in the school and the classroom, but they also took active steps to enhance involvement:

RESEARCH QUOTATION

'...[CoZi teachers] *engaged significantly more in actual outreach activities to bring parents into the school. The CoZi model is designed to change the culture of the school to support a link between home and school and an understanding between parents and teachers; here, it seemed to have done just that.*'

Desimone et al., 2000, pp. 309–310

We do not know the extent to which the teachers' positive attitudes in the CoZi school – described as receptive and supportive – were a cause or an outcome of increased parental participation, or a combination of both. However, it is likely that this finding (increased parental participation) is associated with Barbara Rogoff's comments on the value of professionals being open-minded during their interactions with parents, and avoiding making pre-judgements about the practices and cultural values of families whose backgrounds may differ from their own.

Despite the hardships experienced by the families at the CoZi school, good levels of home–school collaboration were achieved. Perhaps one of the most important aspects of this study was the manner in which parents became active participants in the management of the school. Rather than parental involvement comprising a list of isolated activities, parents engaged collaboratively with teachers and contributed to core decision-making processes at the school, and this was facilitated at an organizational level. The importance of parents' active participation in school management at the CoZi school links with Sheldon and Voorhis' (2004) finding that schools with higher quality partnership schemes had more parental participation on school decision-making committees. Elizabeth Erwin and Leslie Soodak comment on this aspect of parental engagement. They provide an exceptionally useful account of evolving practice in family engagement in the United States, emphasizing the importance of parents not just being 'informed participants' but having genuinely collaborative relationships with professionals. Erwin and Soodak also propose that we should refer to 'family–professional' relationships in recognition of the fact that grandparents and other family members play a significant role in children's education (Erwin and Soodak, 2008).

The CoZi research is of particular relevance because of the characteristics and needs of the families that participated in this study. The CoZi school was located in an area of marked disadvantage, serving single-parent families with very low incomes – members of such a group may experience difficulties in engaging with schools and have traditionally been viewed as hard to reach.

From 'school-centric' to 'parent-centric' ways of viewing involvement: supporting children's mathematics – the United States

In another US initiative, Jackson and Remillard (2005) argue that it is important for schools to shift from what they call 'school-centric' ways of viewing parental involvement (i.e. involvement that is more noticeable and visible) to 'parent-centric' perspectives (i.e. becoming more aware of concealed family practices that support children's learning). These authors investigated how eight African American mothers and two grandmothers from a low-income area viewed their roles in supporting their children's mathematics learning at elementary school (the children were aged approximately 6 to 12). Within the area of parental involvement, few studies have examined how parents

spontaneously support their children's mathematics learning. The authors comment that mathematics education in the United States has recently undergone a number of reforms which have resulted in less of a focus on learning isolated facts and rules and more emphasis on conceptual understanding and problem solving. As with the reforms in mathematics teaching in the United Kingdom, for some parents these developments have resulted in aspects of the curriculum being unfamiliar, and this may have undermined parental confidence in helping children. Within this context, the authors examined parents' and grandparents' approaches when they helped their children with mathematics learning at home, examining whether or not their practices indicated a lack of interest as typically depicted in the literature.

All ten participants (mothers and grandmothers) in this study were living in a low-income community. Their ways of helping their children did not routinely resemble 'school-centric' definitions of involvement, that is, actions that were evident to the school such as volunteering to help in the classroom or attending school-based events. Although some of the parents helped at school, most of the support strategies identified in this study occurred in children's homes. The authors present a framework for examining parental involvement that demonstrates how parents act as **intellectual resources** for their children's learning. Table 3.1 presents the variety of

Table 3.1 Practices that demonstrate how parents and grandmothers act as intellectual resources for their children's learning (adapted from Jackson and Remillard, 2005).

Type of involvement (parents and grandmothers)	What parents/grandmothers do, and the values and perspectives that underpin such actions
Acting as advocates for children's education	Expressing high aspirations for their children. Thinking proactively and strategically about children's futures and the kinds of opportunities that children should experience. Emphasizing the importance of developing children's independence and self-reliance by involving children in household tasks such as washing clothes and cooking.

(Continued)

Table 3.1 (*Continued*)

Type of involvement (parents and grandmothers)	What parents/grandmothers do, and the values and perspectives that underpin such actions
Monitoring children's progress in school	Knowing what children are doing at school and which aspects of the curriculum are causing difficulties.
	Developing strategies for obtaining information about children's progress at school, for example by volunteering to help in class at school.
	Monitoring children's learning by helping with their homework. Making contact with the teacher when their child struggles with an aspect of homework.
Help with homework	Using developed routines such as encouraging children to work independently before seeking assistance.
Planned learning opportunities out of school	Providing a variety of planned opportunities for children's learning, and became extensively involved in these. Some opportunities were spontaneous and developed from household routines such as calculating how much cutlery to use when laying the table, asking a child to find the total for monthly bills, weighing ingredients when cooking or counting money.
	Other learning opportunities included game-like activities that were deliberately introduced to develop mathematical skills such as working out calendar dates.
Obtaining educational materials	Purchasing educational materials to support the children's schoolwork, such as computer software and board games (e.g. Monopoly).

approaches that were adopted by the mothers and grandmothers in Jackson and Remillard's research.

The authors did not claim that the parents and grandmothers in their study were necessarily representative of other African American mothers. Nevertheless, this research throws light on the marked extent to which family members engaged with their children's learning at home in a range of practices. It is apparent that this form of engagement reflects aspects of sociocultural theory, particularly the collaborative nature of learning and the role played by parents and grandmothers in scaffolding children's mathematical understanding.

Another important factor highlighted by this research is the likelihood that such patterns of engagement may well not be evident to teachers, as they tend to occur out of school. It is apparent that the mothers and grandmothers in this study went out of their way to support their children's mathematics learning at home, and that their actions were deliberate and creative. The authors suggest that knowledge of these approaches should help schools to recognize, encourage and build on such practices. They argue that it is essential to distinguish between parental involvement in children's **schooling** and parental involvement in children's **learning** at home, which may be less visible to teachers. This study suggests that the 'unseen' (to schools), home-based support offered by parents with limited financial resources may comprise a key form of parental involvement, and the authors argue that by taking a 'parent-centric' view of involvement parents are recognized as intellectual and educational resources for their children 'beyond the boundaries of schools'.

Learning stories and the assessment of young children with special needs – New Zealand

Traditional assessment approaches adopted by professionals that focus on identifying de-contextualized skills can act as a barrier to parental involvement. Williamson et al. (2006) describe a 'learning story' approach to assessment for young children with severe and complex needs. This approach was developed in New Zealand and it holds considerable promise for including parents in this process.

This approach highlights facilitating factors in children's development and emphasizes the importance of recognizing children's strengths. The learning story approach was initially devised by Margaret Carr (2001) in her book *Assessment in Early Childhood Settings: Learning Stories*.

Williamson et al. explain that in New Zealand, despite the emphasis on early years professionals working in partnership with families, parents continue to feel that they do not make a significant contribution to the assessment and planning processes, and that an 'expert model' that comprises a skills-based approach to assessment tends to typify practice. In contrast, a learning story approach emphasizes the importance of taking account of children's natural environments and the wide range of naturally occurring factors that support children's development, including help from parents and other family members. This is an assessment style which is described by Williamson et al. as holistic, naturalistic and strength based. Table 3.2 illustrates the differences between a traditional, skills-based approach to assessment and a learning stories approach.

In Williamson et al.'s study, parents of two 4-year-old children with complex needs and education support workers were asked to bring written notes or 'narratives' of the child to individual planning meetings. This helped to place parents and support workers on a more equal footing with specialist professionals, who typically bring their own written records to such events. The assessment team included parents, teachers, education support workers, a physiotherapist, a neuro-developmental therapist and speech therapists. The team members were supported for three months by an early childhood professional, and were given guidance on how to write learning stories, which describe factors such as effective teaching approaches, the child's interests, strengths, adult–child relationships and environmental contexts. Learning stories concentrate on what children can do in particular contexts, and on factors that support development. An excerpt from the neuro-developmental therapist's learning story gives a flavour of this form of assessment: 'Each time Ben threw a ball correctly the two adults standing either side of him, myself and dad, clapped and cheered. Ben raised his arms in the air each time and called out "yea" with a big grin – ear to ear. Ben was able to maintain a stable base whilst throwing the balls overhead from 80 cm in front of the box' (Williamson et al., 2006, p. 25). A comment from a parent in this study underlines the extent to which she appreciated that her

Table 3.2　Skills-based and learning story approaches to assessment (based on Williamson et al., 2006).

Skills-based approach to assessment	Learning story approach to assessment
May take place in an unfamiliar setting (e.g. a clinic), using materials/toys chosen by an adult.	Observation occurs in children's natural environments (children's homes, nurseries, etc.), using artefacts the child chooses to play with/use.
Focuses on deficits or gaps in learning, on skills acquired (e.g. being able to pick up objects with a pincer-like grasp), and on the next skill to be taught.	Concentrates on the child's strengths and interests, and on factors that help children learn.
Splits up the child into different domains (e.g. language/communication; cognitive development; social skills).	Is holistic and emphasizes the interconnectedness between areas or processes such as the child's personality, how the child chooses to communicate, the child's health, etc. The child is viewed as a whole person.
Administered by specialists.	Can be administered by non-specialists.
De-emphasizes parents' contribution.	View parents' perspectives as equally valid to those of professionals.
Drawn from professional knowledge and training.	Reflects current early childhood philosophies and practice.
Uses specialist language that can exclude parents.	Adopts a common language that is used by all, including parents and support workers.
Expertise is confined to specialist professionals.	Expertise is shared between professionals, parents, other family members and support workers – the role of 'expert' is distributed, and all ideas are valued. Parents, teachers and support workers are more involved in the process.

contribution was valued and was accorded a similar weighting to that of professionals:

RESEARCH QUOTATION

'With Learning Stories everyone is on a level playing field. If they had been in place at the start then we wouldn't have been struggling with all the different languages they [the professionals] used. If these had been around right from the start they would have eased a lot of stress.'

Williamson et al., 2006, p. 25

Williamson et al. comment that a challenge for early intervention professionals is to emphasize children's interests, strengths and contexts for learning, and to give less weight to de-contextualized information on developmental skills. Practices that concentrate on listing children's skills without reference to contextual factors and practices that result in learning goals that may not take account of holistic factors such as children's interests and preferences may inhibit parental contributions to assessment and planning processes. This may be exacerbated when assessment reports are written using specialist language or jargon, which may be particularly intimidating for parents for whom English is not their first language and for parents who may not have the confidence to ask for clarification. Although Williamson et al.'s study explores the involvement of parents with young children with complex and severe needs, there are important implications for involving parents in assessment practices generally. It is likely that many parents – including those with older children who experience a range of difficulties – would welcome the use of learning stories to help in the presentation of a holistic perspective that is valued by assessment specialists, and would feel that they were contributing on a more equal basis.

Another innovative example of early years practice where parents' perspectives are strongly endorsed comes from northern Italy.

The Reggio Emilia approach to early years education – Italy

Reggio Emilia is a town in the north of Italy where the philosophy and practices developed in centres for pre-school children over the last half century have attracted increasing international interest. Scott (2001) identifies some of the core beliefs that typify the Reggio Emilia approach, many of which characterize traditional nursery education in the United Kingdom, that is, practices which are underpinned by a child-centred philosophy and which use children's own initiatives as the foundation for learning:

RESEARCH QUOTATION

'Staff in the centres recognize and celebrate the many ways young children represent their ideas. The importance of paying attention to what children say, and uncovering what they mean, is a key part of the approach to early education in Reggio Emilia . . . The community shares a strong belief that children are rich and powerful learners, deserving of respect.'

Scott, 2001, p. 22

The ethos behind the Reggio Emilia approach has been strongly influenced by aspects of sociocultural theory developed by Vygotsky and Bruner. For example, in order to enhance children's learning, staff in the centres are keen to build on the interactive relationships developed between children and their immediate and extended families. The pedagogical style used in the centres reflects a collaborative, exploratory approach between adults and children, characterized by reciprocity and reflection (Edwards, 2003).

What is of particular interest in the Reggio Emilia approach is the high level of parental involvement. This stems from a range of historical and cultural factors that contributed to the development of these pre-school centres. After World War II, increasing numbers of the Italian population migrated from the relatively poor south to the north, where employment prospects were better. As women moved into the workplace, parents sought high-quality childcare. Parents wanted to find alternatives to the strict, church-dominated approach adopted in pre-school centres that was characteristic of early education at that time (LeBlanc, 2008). They were also determined to find alternatives to the Fascist ideology that dominated Italian culture during the war years, and were keen to develop early years provision on the basis of democratic, inclusive values (Scott, 2001). The parents were helped by Loris Malaguzzi, an elementary school teacher, thought to be the pedagogical founder of the Reggio Emilia approach (Thornton and

Brunton, 2005). It was parents who founded the pre-school centres in Reggio Emilia, not the state, and this contributed to parental involvement being at the very heart of the centres' educational philosophy, both practically and in terms of core values (New, 2007).

Wendy Scott, an English teacher living in Reggio Emilia, describes her experience as a parent, emphasizing the extent to which parental skills and knowledge are valued, and how the flexibility and availability of educators facilitate parent/teacher relationships:

RESEARCH QUOTATION

'*All the parents* [of children attending Reggio Emilia centres] *were encouraged to bring whatever skills or interests they may have to school for the benefit of the environment and the enhancement of our common experience . . . Flexible entry and leaving times meant that the teachers were happy and available to chat and exchange information . . . Parents were encouraged to become closely involved in school life; class, parent and teacher meetings were held regularly and parent participation and observations greatly encouraged lively discussion.*'

Scott, 2001, p. 39

Jenny Leask, a parent of a child aged 7 months who attended a Reggio Emilia pre-school during the mornings, describes the measures taken to ensure that parents' perspectives play a central role:

RESEARCH QUOTATION

'*The teachers were always ready to talk and listen at the beginning and end of the day and there were daily running records showing what Sam had had for lunch, his bodily functions (riveting reading) and the activities the group had been involved in during the day . . . Over the course of the year written panels appeared at both child and adult height in Sam's room documenting with words and photographs moments in the children's learning – observations of work in progress. These panels are incredibly affecting in their projection of your own or someone else's child as protagonists in their own learning.*'

Leask, 2001, p. 45

Jenny Leask comments on her surprise at the extent to which the teachers valued her and her husband's contribution. She notes that parents' evenings were frequent (three or four per term, always illustrated by photographs or videos of the children at work or on outings), usually started after 9 p.m. and 'always go on until well after midnight', presumably to facilitate participation by working parents. She describes the ways in which she and her husband could choose to be involved at a practical level (e.g. being a helper during a trip or repairing centre equipment) or at an administrative level (by contributing to school meetings addressing policy and education matters, and so forth). The Reggio Emilia approach clearly made a significant impact on this family: 'I think that our experiences as parents . . . have profoundly changed our ideas and expectations regarding children, adults and parents learning together in the community of school' (Leask, 2001, p. 47).

The Reggio centres adopt a number of practical approaches for welcoming parents and making them feel at ease at school when their child first starts. Many early years centres in the United Kingdom organize workshops and other sessions for parents during this important period. However, what is of particular interest in the Reggio centres is that rather than focusing on teaching and other matters, educators see this as an opportunity to learn from parents. Linda Thornton and Pat Brunton (2005) explain that a key aim of the induction programme offered to parents of children who join the centres is to explore parents' outlooks: 'The programme is planned to make the family feel at home and a part of the structure, and to give educators the opportunity to talk with the parents and to begin to understand the parent's unique perspective of their own child' (p. 51). Furthermore, in prospectuses given to parents, a detailed plan of the centre's ground floor is included to help parents become acquainted with and feel more confident about the place where their child is educated (Thornton and Brunton, 2005).

Reggio centres have much to offer parents of young children, including children with special educational needs. In Italy children who are described as having special educational needs are those whose difficulties would be called 'severe' in the United Kingdom. The term 'special educational needs' in Italy does **not** refer to the much wider group of children with a range of lower level difficulties, which in the United Kingdom would be around 20%. This term (special educational needs) is applied to around 1.7% of the Italian school population, that is, roughly the proportion of children who in the United Kingdom are educated in special schools (Phillips, 2001). It is worth bearing this in mind when considering the level and type of support provided for such children in Reggio Emilia pre-school centres. For if a child is identified as having special educational needs, then Italian law stipulates that the class size should not exceed 20, and a specialist teacher is allocated to support the child (Phillips, 2001). This is an innovative approach to supporting children in mainstream settings and provides relatively generous levels of resourcing (compared with the United Kingdom).

In 1994 the 'Reggio Children Organization' was established to facilitate educational and cultural exchange initiatives between early childhood services and teachers and researchers from across the world. More information about this organization and about Reggio centres can be found at www.reggiochildren.it.

Conclusions

A distinct and recurrent topic that emerges in the perspectives and projects discussed in this chapter is that positive teacher attitudes towards harder to reach parents matter immensely – attitudes that avoid the formation of value judgements and that include respectful acknowledgement of parental practices at home that are supportive of children's learning. This raises the question of how such positive teacher attitudes can be fostered. A well-known (and counter-intuitive) adage in the field of educational intervention is that behaviour change often precedes attitude change. In other words, the most effective way to engender a change of outlook may be to first change what people **do** – once individuals start behaving differently, new ways of viewing the world can often ensue. However, the knowledge that behaviour change may need to come before attitude change does not provide a definitive answer to one of the dilemmas facing those who want to develop more successful connections between schools and homes. This is a dilemma which encompasses a question of directionality: do positive staff attitudes towards parents result in better home–school links? Or, is it the other way round – do better home–school links produce more positive staff attitudes?

It seems likely that a combination of both takes place and that this process is two way and interactive.

The four projects that have been outlined in this chapter include practical examples for schools to consider when developing links with parents who might seem harder to reach. Although schools with a positive and inclusive ethos towards parental involvement may be better positioned to develop such approaches, it is likely that the process of active engagement with the sorts of initiatives presented will in itself bring about positive attitudes.

4

Successful Projects in the United Kingdom

Introduction

In this chapter, we discuss a range of small-to-medium projects that have been developed and evaluated in the United Kingdom. The commentary does not include reference to larger scale (national) projects such as *Sure Start* and *Family Learning*, as information about such initiatives is available on web sites: www.surestart.gov.uk and www.campaign-for-learning.org.uk.

The approaches presented here have been selected for a number of reasons. As with the schemes discussed in Chapter 3, the design and focus of these approaches make them particularly relevant for schools working with harder to reach parents. This may be due to the fact that the projects were developed in areas characterized by poverty, where there exist various constraints on families that make it more difficult for parents to liaise closely with teachers. These approaches include examples where non-deficit approaches to involving parents were deliberately adopted and where schools recognized that families had much to offer their children. They also included forms of adaptation on the part of staff, where schools recognized the needs of families and

Engaging 'Hard to Reach' Parents: Teacher–Parent Collaboration to Promote Children's Learning By Anthony Feiler © 2010 John Wiley & Sons, Ltd

made adjustments to accommodate such needs. The initiatives each contain features that can be readily taken on by staff, or adapted and developed so that they fit a range of different contexts and different situations. The projects used inventive, imaginative approaches to parental involvement where ingenuity and sensitivity mattered more than large amounts of funding.

The Letterbox Club

In Chapter 2 one of the most perturbing issues raised was the low educational achievement of looked-after children. The government report *Care Matters* (Department for Education and Skills, 2006) presents a worrying account of the poor progress made by many children in care at school: stark differences in achievement exist at all ages, and at the age of 15–16 years the proportion of looked-after children attaining good GCSEs in 2005 was five times less than other children. The long-term outcomes are equally worrisome: children who have been in care are less likely than other young people to be in training after the age of 16, and are more likely to become teenage parents, unemployed, drug users and imprisoned. The report highlighted five key reasons why looked-after children underachieve:

Instability: looked-after children frequently experience a change in care placement, which can trigger a change of school.

Less time spent in school: young people in care spend too much time out of school or other places of learning.

Insufficient help with education: children in care need more support with education when they fall behind.

Insufficient support and encouragement: carers are not expected or equipped to provide adequate levels of support and encouragement at home for learning and development.

Insufficient emotional support: children in care need more help with their mental or physical health and well-being.

Approximately two-thirds of looked-after children live with foster parents, and the remainder mostly live in children's homes or with their parents whilst being the subject of a care order (Social Exclusion

Unit, 2003). Foster parents can play an immensely important role in supporting the education of children in care. The *Letterbox Club* presents a practical approach for improving educational outcomes for children aged 7–11 who are looked after by foster families. This scheme was instigated by Rose Griffiths at the University of Leicester's School of Education and is managed by Booktrust (www.booktrust.org.uk).

During the early stages of this initiative, a pilot project was developed for children in foster care attending four schools. One of the pioneering approaches used in this creative scheme was to supply resources direct to children. This decision was taken because it emerged from interviews with a sample group of foster carers, before the start of the project, that although some of the foster carers welcomed the option of helping their foster children at home with reading or mathematics, others were less enthusiastic. Some foster parents expressed a lack of confidence about their role in supporting children's learning or anticipated that the children would not be motivated to participate. So it was agreed that books and other materials would be sent straight to the children by post in personally addressed packages, and the children were free to decide whether to use them and whether or not to share them with others in the foster home. There was no expectation that foster parents had to be involved. The goal of the project was to improve the children's attitude and attainment in literacy and numeracy; in addition, the scheme aimed to increase the children's foster parents' confidence in helping learn at home.

Before the *Letterbox Club* project started, one foster parent expressed reservations about children receiving posted materials as this might result in one of her foster children receiving letters from members of his family who were prohibited from making contact. So the materials were sent in red envelopes with 'Letterbox Club' stickers on them. During the initial stages of the project, each parcel contained one or two books (fiction, poetry or non-fiction), a mathematics activity and any necessary stationery items for tackling these activities such as scissors or glue. The packages were sent once a month for 6 months. In each packet, there was also a letter personally addressed to the child. The children's attainment in reading and mathematics was assessed at the start of the project, and the books and mathematics activities that were subsequently sent were chosen according to the children's age and level of achievement. One of the parcels contained a cassette tape to accompany a storybook, and this proved to be very popular. Mathematics games were also well liked, as were the sheets of personalized name labels with the message, 'This book belongs to . . .', and the child's name inserted.

In terms of outcomes, 20 children aged 7–11 and their foster parents and teachers participated in a pilot evaluation of this scheme. For the nine children who were still at primary school at the end of the pilot phase, five of the children made better progress with reading than they had previously (three of the children made gains in their reading ages of 14, 16 and 18 months). Six of the nine children showed improvements in mathematics. Several children referred to the significance of opening a personally addressed *Letterbox Club* package, commenting that it was the first time they had ever received a letter or parcel.

A number of minor difficulties were noted by the author of this project. None of the children joined the local library, even though library membership forms and leaflets were included in three of the six parcels. Griffiths suggests that for future work it may be worthwhile sending children a library ticket (not just a library form) and information about specific library events. It also proved difficult to find suitable books and other materials that matched the children's interest and attainment levels.

Booktrust and the University of Leicester received support from the Department for Children, Schools and Families and sponsorship from Penguin for a national pilot project in 2007 and 2008; the interim report for the year 2007 showing the benefits of reading, mathematics and children's interest in learning is available on www.letterboxclub.org.uk. At the time of writing, over 4500 children from all over the United Kingdom have been registered to be members of the *Letterbox Club* for 2009. Further information about *The Letterbox Club* can be found on www.booktrust.org.uk and www.letterboxclub.org.uk.

'Drop in for Coffee': working with parents in North Perth new community schools

The notion of schools offering a broader range of services to families evolved in the United States during the early 1980s and was initiated in response to educational underachievement in disadvantaged areas

(The Scottish Office, 1998). This development recognizes that services need to adopt more holistic approaches in providing support for children and young people's educational, social, emotional and physical needs, and that schools cannot solve the problems associated with social exclusion and deprivation on their own (Wilkin et al., 2003). Karayiannis (2006) points out that the concept of school as a community resource is becoming increasingly acceptable internationally: like 'Full Service Schools' in the United States, Sweden has 'Open' schools, and Canada has 'School Plus'. The UK government is currently encouraging schools to become more extended in order to build stronger relationships with parents and the wider community (Department for Education and Skills, 2004d, 2007b). Dyson and Robson (1999) propose that schools that offer more extended services to families and the community should function as a resource for the community rather than viewing the community as a resource to the school. They also propose that in responding to the needs of the community, staff need to see this role as the core purpose of the school, not 'as a distraction'.

In Scotland, Integrated Community Schools are encouraged to work closely with other agencies in order to reduce social exclusion. The aim of the Integrated Community Schools initiative is to provide education, health and welfare services to parents and children under one institution, that is, the school (Tett, 2005). The aspirations of this development are strongly rooted in the field of social justice and seem formidably demanding. However, accounts of specific, practical projects are beginning to emerge, and these provide an insight into how such ambitions might be realized. One such example is an inspiring project – the *Drop in for Coffee* scheme – described by Illsley and Redford (2005). One of the key aims of Integrated Community Schools in Scotland is to enhance engagement with families and the wider community. The *Drop in for Coffee* scheme was developed in a group of Scotland's Integrated Community Schools and centres in North Perth, and the key aspects are listed below:

- Parents were invited to 'drop in' for coffee in pre-school, primary and secondary schools.
- The initial approaches and invitations to parents (e.g. by teachers or community learning workers) were deliberately informal and were made in playgrounds, when parents dropped off their children at schools/nurseries, or during parents' evenings. Illsley

and Redford (2005) report that when one of the mothers was approached about joining this project she commented, 'I don't do groups, but I'll come for a quick coffee.' This mother remained with the project for 3 years and has since addressed conferences about the impact the coffee groups made on her life.

- The numbers in the *Drop in for Coffee* groups (usually mothers) varied from 6 to 12, with creche provision for four to six young children or babies.

- The groups decided on their own programme of activities and these included art and crafts, healthy cooking and inviting head teachers to discuss issues such as secondary transfer.

- Subsequent groups (*Coffee Too* and *Coffee Extra*) supported further personal development amongst the parents including computer skills, literacy and numeracy, and creative writing. Various accredited certificate courses were offered – the majority of parents who originally 'dropped in' subsequently progressed to adult education, volunteering or family learning opportunities.

- All the groups were held in schools, nurseries or children's service centres (typically where education, social work and health services are brought together on one site). The authors note: 'The informality of the groups has contributed to the development of the shared space. School staff often took the opportunity to come into a *Drop in for Coffee* group to say hello to parents, taste any food made, admire crafts produced or simply have a coffee or a piece of fruit' (Illsley and Redford, 2005, p. 164).

In an (unpublished) evaluation of this project, a head teacher observed that parents were more willing to speak with her because she participated in the *Drop in for Coffee* group, whereas previously they had hardly lifted their heads when they saw her approaching (Humphris, 2004, cited in Illsley and Redford, 2005). It is likely that the informality of the *Drop in for Coffee* groups contributed to parental engagement, helping to put families at ease and to overcome feelings of apprehension. The authors emphasize that many parents had negative experiences when they themselves attended school, had not achieved academic success and had no formal qualifications. The project demonstrates a thoughtful approach to involving parents, offering support to families in a highly sensitive manner that was deliberately designed to avoid embarrassment or discomfort. It offered parents the opportunity to extend their range of knowledge and skills and brought together professionals from a range of agencies. Tett (2005) notes that Integrated Community Schools in Scotland have concentrated particularly on socially excluded families, who experience a range of difficulties including poverty, poor housing and health and low educational attainment. Such difficulties can present severe challenges not only to the families but also to teachers and other professionals who offer support. An important aspect of the work of Integrated Community Schools is that school staff are not expected to undertake this work in isolation. Tett (2005) emphasizes that one of the strengths of working in this way is that no single agency is left to respond to the complex range of difficulties such families face.

INSPIRE: involving school parents in reading and mathematics

Beryl Bateson (2000) presents an engaging overview of the INSPIRE initiative (involving school parents in reading and mathematics). The scale of this project marks it out from many other parental involvement initiatives: INSPIRE was developed across the 370 primary and nursery schools in Birmingham, and was aimed at involving all parents, rather than being targeted at specific groups judged to be in need of help.

Strong support for INSPIRE was provided by Birmingham Local Authority. This backing had its roots in an earlier Local Authority focus on adult learning. It was recognized within the authority that those with low levels of basic skills in literacy and numeracy were more likely to experience social exclusion and to be unemployed or employed in low-paid unskilled jobs, and were more likely to be homeless or to offend. In order to improve levels of literacy and numeracy in Birmingham, the Core Skills Development Partnership (www.coreskills.co.uk) was formed in 1996. It consisted of various city council departments and voluntary services as well as the national Basic Skills Agency. The aim of this initiative was to improve literacy and numeracy skills across all communities and age groups in Birmingham. A key goal was to engage parents and families in literacy and numeracy learning. This gave an important boost to the development of the INSPIRE programme with its focus on families with children attending primary schools.

Staff working on the INSPIRE scheme recognized that negative judgements and assumptions can prevail about what parents can offer. The INSPIRE project aimed to change the beliefs and attitudes of teachers and other professionals working with parents, as well as parents themselves, in order to raise expectations:

RESEARCH QUOTATION

'Many acknowledged that parents often do not have the confidence to be involved in school or to help in their children's education; that they may have had bad experiences in education themselves; that they may not have had access to knowledge on how to be involved or that they needed their information to be updated; and that not all teachers or all schools make it easy for them to be involved. These barriers run alongside practical difficulties such as no available accommodation in school, little non-contact time for teachers, no child-care facilities for younger siblings and, with some families, no common language with which to communicate. And so we had to INSPIRE school staff that involving parents really could make a difference and it really is worth making this a priority . . . Teachers in turn had to INSPIRE parents and families about the value of what is done or can be done at home that supports the child's learning.'

Bateson, 2000, p. 56

The challenge for INSPIRE workers was to convince staff working in schools that parents from a range of social and cultural backgrounds could be productively involved in education and that this would have a significant impact on children's learning. Similarly, those who devised this scheme set out to convince and inspire parents that they could be constructively involved with their child's learning. Bateson (2000) lists the following aims of INSPIRE:

- To achieve more effective partnerships between schools and home.
- To enhance and increase opportunities for learning in and through the home.
- For schools to share with parents information about teaching and learning in school.
- To contribute to raising achievement in literacy and mathematics.

The core features of INSPIRE are presented below (Bateson, 2000);

- A day's training conducted by the Local Authority is offered to head teachers, other senior staff and teachers.
- Each school plans and prepares a school-based parental involvement workshop, focusing on one class at a time. A trained mentor is available for schools during early stages – mentors are teachers with experience in using INSPIRE, with paid release from the Authority to support schools that are new to the scheme.
- Children in the target class are asked to invite a special adult – for example a parent, grandparent, neighbour or a family friend – to the school to support them during the school-based workshop.
- Teachers write to parents about the forthcoming event, highlighting the importance of someone from the family attending the workshop. Staff may speak individually to some parents and may make telephone contact with others to discuss ways of overcoming any difficulties the family may have in attending.
- The class teacher sets up practical activities for the families based on the literacy or mathematics curriculum, often linked to a specific target in the National Literacy or Numeracy Framework.
- The parents (or extended family members or other special adults), whilst waiting in the school hall or spare classroom (or wherever the workshop is to be held), are warmly welcomed by the school staff. It has been found that the best time to hold the workshop is either when children are first dropped off at the school in the morning, or after lunch during the first session of the afternoon.
- The invited adult sits next to the child in the classroom when practical, fun activities are introduced (such as making a game, singing a song or working with puppets).
- At the start of the workshop, the teacher explains what activities will be presented and what is the adults' role (either before the children come in or in the presence of children). Preparation with the children before this event tends to be effective in generating their interest and enthusiasm (e.g. showing them the masks, puppets or games they will be making, or practising rhymes or songs).
- The invited adult and child then gather various materials from around the room and, with the help of staff and helpers, start the activities. A choice of practical tasks is presented, and families can take materials home.

- One teacher in each school has a designated responsibility for managing and coordinating INSPIRE activities.
- INSPIRE makes links with other family learning programmes such as *Family Literacy* (www.literacytrust.org.uk), *Bookstart* (www.bookstart.co.uk), *Flying Start* (http://services.bgfl.org/services) and *Early Start* (www.literacytrust.org.uk).

It is worth noting that schools are not given prescribed lessons or materials to deliver, and the focus of workshops is not seen as training for parents:

> **RESEARCH QUOTATION**
>
> *'INSPIRE is offered purely as an opportunity for parents/carers to work with their child alongside the teachers and be involved in activities that support their child. This is what we believe parents really do want.'*
>
> Bateson, 2000, p. 56

Birmingham has many deprived areas with relatively large numbers of black and minority ethnic groups whose first language is not English. INSPIRE included not only those parents who were from more affluent areas of the city but also those from disadvantaged areas whose involvement with the school had not been extensive – parents who had not traditionally been strongly involved in education. Evaluation data indicate strong support from staff and parents, and the scheme was successful in attracting very high numbers of families across the city of Birmingham. INSPIRE developed links with a wide range of organizations delivering services to families in hostels and refuges:

> **RESEARCH QUOTATION**
>
> *'These developments [INSPIRE] have recently been extended to include support for families in hostels and refuges. In the first six months a total of 156 parents and 204 children in 12 hostels have worked through a mix of workshops, short courses and book sharing sessions . . . The activities are supported by book loans within the hostels and encouragement for families to use the local libraries.'*
>
> www.coreskills.co.uk

The INSPIRE framework is applicable to schools in a wide range of contexts, and as the approach is strongly rooted in the National Curriculum, it does not undermine teachers' main priority – their pupils' learning. The uncomplicated structure of this practical model renders its approach both flexible and robust. It should be noted that despite INSPIRE's straightforwardness it is a model underpinned by carefully considered and well thought-through principles such as giving children an empowering role in choosing who to invite to school and using activity-based learning to give parents and others access to the curriculum.

The Home–School Knowledge Exchange project

The Home–School Knowledge Exchange (HSKE) project was carried out between 2001 and 2005 by staff based mainly at the Graduate School of Education, University of Bristol. It was funded by the Economic and Social Research Council, and directed by Professor Martin Hughes. The author was a member of the research team that conducted this work; part of the work has been described in *Improving Primary Literacy: Linking Home and School* (Feiler et al., 2007). The account that follows has been taken from Feiler et al. (2006, 2008).

The HSKE project was based on the following supposition: parents and teachers have knowledge that is relevant to enhancing children's learning and this knowledge is often poorly communicated and under-utilized. Interventions involving parents may fail to recognize the skills and the approaches that they adopt and can result in school values and practices being imposed on less advantaged families (Hughes and Pollard, 2006). A key principle that influenced the design and implementation of the HSKE project was the desire to recognize and build on existing home practices, helping schools to become more sensitive to families' social capital and fostering links through the development of bridging mechanisms between families and teachers. As discussed in Chapter 2, the work of Luis Moll and other researchers (Moll et al., 1992) suggests that all families possess extensive 'funds of knowledge', including those who live in deprived or disadvantaged circumstances. The HKSE project aimed to develop knowledge exchange activities that would enable parents to make a valued and significant contribution to their children's learning, based on their funds of knowledge. This might include knowledge of how their children approach learning, what motivates them, what children know and what they would like to find out about. The corollary to the recognition that families have 'funds of knowledge' is that teachers too have a wealth of knowledge about the range of subjects that comprise the curriculum and about children's learning at school. Although teachers know a great deal about pedagogy and the content of the curriculum, they may know little about children's out-of-school worlds. Similarly, although parents know much about children's home interests, their skills and what they find exciting, they may know little about the content and teaching of curriculum subjects such as literacy and mathematics. The core goal of the HSKE project was to enable teachers and parents to pool their funds of knowledge in order to enhance children's learning.

There were three 'strands' of the HSKE project:

- Developing literacy at Key Stage 1 (children aged 5–7 years).
- Developing numeracy at Key Stage 2 (children aged 7–11 years).
- Facilitating transfer between primary and secondary schools (children aged 11–12 years).

Within each of the three 'strands', researchers on the HSKE project worked in four primary schools – two in Bristol and two in Cardiff – developing, implementing and evaluating a range of knowledge exchange activities. These were the actions designed to bring home and school together more closely, helping parents and teachers to share their knowledge of children's learning. In each city, one of the primary schools had higher proportions of children eligible for free school meals with the other school having lower proportions. In general, the socio-economic range represented in the schools with a lower proportion of children eligible for free school meals was generally mixed but included a majority of middle-class families; whilst the schools with a higher proportion of children eligible for free school meals represented low socio-economic status populations. The schools' intakes reflected the ethnic diversity present in the two cities. The activities presented below illustrate approaches for enhancing literacy and numeracy learning. The activities were selected on the basis that they involved parents whom schools might find, for a variety of reasons, more challenging to engage and who might be described as harder to reach. The discussion below has been taken from Feiler et al. (2006).

Using video to communicate with parents about literacy and numeracy teaching strategies

There is a tendency for teachers to communicate with families in writing. However, using print to communicate can prove problematic for some parents, as one mother in the HSKE project indicated: 'I didn't [learn to read] until I was 11, I have to say . . . we used to do the Peter and Jane books and I used to take them home and my sister used to read them to me and I used to memorize them, so that's how they never picked up that I couldn't read . . . but there you go, I can now.'

Even where parents are able to read English, they may be disinclined to access information through this medium. One parent who participated in the HSKE project, who acquired English reading skills late, explained how she used the social network of parents waiting in the playground to determine the content of letters: 'when I go up to school there's usually a few of us and we all talk, "Okay, did anybody read that letter? Can somebody translate, so I don't have to read it?" . . . and then they put the input, "Well I think it's about" and I go, "Okay then", and off I go.'

In order to avoid an over-reliance on the written word, alternative strategies were developed for communicating with parents. A prime example was the use of video. At the start of the HSKE project, parents had expressed a desire to know more about the ways their children were taught in school. Videos were made of literacy lessons in all four of the schools, and of mathematics teaching approaches in two of the schools. Copies of the video were made for each family in case parents were unable to attend the school-based screenings that were arranged. The individual copies were accompanied by a booklet which included aspects the teacher wanted to highlight and ideas for helping children at home.

The highest turnouts for the video screenings (with around three-quarters of parents attending) were at the schools with lower proportions of children eligible for free school meals. One of these schools provided the only evening viewing. It was very well attended and included several fathers. The teacher at this school was surprised by the high turnout and also by which parents came (i.e. parents of a number of lower achieving children). At one school, in addition to sending out written invitations, the class teacher personally invited parents to the screenings during the course of parents' evenings. At the two schools where literacy activities were developed and where there were higher proportions of children eligible for free school meals, slightly less than one-half of parents attended one school-based screening, whilst less than one-third of parents came to the other. These numbers point up the importance of making the video available for viewing at home.

Whilst the literacy videos were edited versions of complete lessons, a different format was used for the numeracy videos. There was a focus on procedures for carrying out calculations and this was a response to the sense of deskilling that parents expressed, which resulted from the use of teaching methods that differed from those used in their own education either in the United Kingdom or in other countries. Two of the mothers commented: 'What confuses me is that they do their calculations slightly different to how we were taught to do them ... I try and show her my way and she says, "Oh, you don't know what you're doing." And I give her answer with my own way, and then ... we does it like a big way, difficult way, and she'll say, "Oh mum, like this way is easier" ... I wish I went to school here, but I didn't.'

English was an additional language for several children in one of the numeracy video classes. In an attempt to make the video as widely accessible as possible to their families, some sequences were recorded in home languages, with students of Pakistani and Bangladeshi heritage working together in groups.

Building on home knowledge – using disposable cameras

There are varied reasons why participation in activities located at school may be difficult for some parents. In addition to language differences, parents may have family responsibilities such as caring for younger children or elderly family members, working hours that coincide with the school day, illness or transport difficulties. Sending video material home may help to overcome some of these barriers. However, it has been argued that focusing on school learning alone can be marginalizing since it excludes children's out-of-school experiences (Caddell et al., 2000).

The HSKE researchers sought to promote the exchange of knowledge between home and school as a two-way process, that is, knowledge flowing from home to school as well as from school to home. They were keen to explore strategies for bringing children's out-of-school worlds into the classroom. Photographs were used as a medium for tackling this, and children were given disposable cameras to use at home over a holiday period. They were asked to take photographs relating to class topics on making a model vehicle, living things, plants and growth and the local environment. Most parents helped their children at home with the photography.

In two of the schools (both with higher proportions of children eligible for free school meals), parents were invited to the school to help the children make a book from captioned photographs. Older siblings were also invited to join these sessions. In both schools, about half the children were supported in class by parents. Since they knew the provenance of the photos and the circumstances in which they were taken, parents developed specialist knowledge and were able to help the children express the meaning of the pictures as well as helping out with the practicalities.

Displaying children's work away from the school location

Some parents can experience feelings of insecurity and discomfort just because of being in a school; such feelings can result from negative experiences they had during their own school days (Whalley, 2001). In one of the HSKE project schools (with higher proportions of children eligible for free school meals), an exhibition of children's work was deliberately displayed away from the school site in a nearby supermarket used by many of the parents. The exhibition included photographs of previous project activities, for example photos of parents and siblings helping to make books from photographs taken at home, and explanations of the activities and other information were provided for parents. The class video of the literacy lesson was also played continuously.

The exhibition was open from 8 a.m. to about 6 p.m. on two consecutive days. Colourful invitations to the exhibition were sent out, which included a voucher for a free cup of tea or coffee at the supermarket's café. It was difficult to keep tabs on the number of class parents who visited, as the place was sometimes very busy with parents from other classes and other members of the community also dropping by, but at least two-thirds of parents attended this event (this was more than double the number of parents attending the original video screening of the literacy lesson at this school).

The response to this activity was very positive, and the pattern of visiting was particularly interesting, with parents making more than a single visit and in different social groupings. For example, one mother of Indian heritage, who had not previously participated in any school-based events, visited with her children twice, and she also visited on her own; the children's paternal grandfather, aunt and cousins also visited. The visiting parents seemed to be at ease in this familiar territory, where expectations regarding school ways of doing things were less evident, and where members of the extended family and next-door neighbours could also take an interest in a child's education.

Discussion of the HSKE project

Although different in form, the activities discussed above were, to a certain extent, characterized by an attempt to see things from the parental or home viewpoint. This endeavour does present difficulties, however, since there may be no common parental viewpoint. Something that suits one family may not suit another. Whilst one mother of Somali heritage suggested that she would like information in her own language so that she could read it independently without having to ask another member of the family to translate it, another parent, again of Somali heritage, commented that she preferred information to be sent home in English so that her daughter could read and translate it.

An implication of this heterogeneity is that schools need to put effort into finding out from parents what kinds of activities and support they would find helpful. However, here again things may not be straightforward. The demands placed on schools by consultation processes that seek to access the views of parents may be quite extensive; and some parents may not have clear views as to what might be envisaged. According to a telephone survey by Williams et al. (2002),

30% of the parents contacted said that they did not know what could be done to get parents more involved in their children's school life.

A further implication of heterogeneity is that when it comes to choosing appropriate activities, one size cannot fit all. Perhaps the best that can be aimed for is to put in place a range of actions that will include different participants at different times in different ways. Whilst such a plan aims for overall coverage, inevitably there will be variation.

In Chapter 2 it is noted that referring to certain families as 'hard to reach' can be problematic, partly because it may divert attention away from the examination of factors within services and institutions that may make these services and institutions difficult to access. This has been considered by the National Literacy Trust, which comments: 'The most disadvantaged people tend not to use services ... Such groups have sometimes been called 'hard to reach'. This is a contentious term and it might be fairer for the services themselves to be called hard to reach' (National Literacy Trust, 2005, p. 80). During the HSKE project, it became apparent that parents from a wide range of social backgrounds were interested in knowing more about how to help their children learn, including those who could be described as disadvantaged. Furthermore, it was apparent that family practices and languages varied and it was important to use a variety of approaches to communicate with parents for fuller family engagement.

One of the most rewarding aspects of this work was the realization that where communication between homes and schools was effective, parents' contribution to their child's learning was often rich and extensive. This occurred with the disposable camera activity. Parents with widely differing means and resources helped their children to record the diversity of their home lives in images that were welcomed by teachers. Schools viewed variations in children's out-of-school lives constructively – difference was transformed into diversity and some parents who might have been viewed as harder to reach engaged actively with their children's learning.

The schools in the HSKE project were helped to undertake some of these activities through the support of the research team. Whilst the materials supplied to schools were not lavish, they included a set of disposable cameras for each participating class and video cameras; schools were also provided with interpreters to attend meetings. With resource constraints in schools, it could be difficult to build this provision into the regular spending of schools. Schools may be able to find alternative sources of funding, possibly from sponsorship by local companies, and Local Authority funding may be available for the provision of interpreters. In addition, developing technology may help reduce costs. With digital cameras becoming less expensive, these might be shared by groups of pupils over a period of time and the costs of film processing will also reduce since selected images can be printed in school. However, in addition to the equipment, there are also costs in terms of time. Aspects such as providing flexible timings for meetings both during the day and in the evening require the teacher's working day to be viewed and structured differently. Here again there are financial implications. Hence, for the full potential of home–school knowledge exchange to be realized, investment will be required.

Five key principles that underpin the process of exchanging knowledge between home and schools to help children learn are listed in Box 4.1.

Box 4.1   Key principles that underpin the process of exchanging knowledge between home and schools to help children learn (taken from Feiler et al., 2007).

- All families possess important 'funds of knowledge' which can be drawn on to enhance children's learning in school.
- Communication needs to take place in two directions, from home to school as well as from school to home.
- Home–school knowledge exchange cannot be imposed in a uniform way. Some excellent ideas that have been tried and tested in one context may not work in other settings, so teachers need to be prepared to amend and adapt ideas.
- Diversity amongst children and families needs to be viewed as an opportunity and not a problem. Exploring the richness of children's home lives can be a highly motivating stimulus for learning in school. With careful planning and classroom organization, the multiplicity of ideas, issues and 'stories' that emanate from 30 individuals can be shared with all.
- It is important to recognize that together with what parents and teachers know, children's own knowledge is at the core of the process of home–school knowledge exchange.

In reporting this study, the researchers tried to avoid the use of an overly positive emphasis that can typify project reporting in the field of parental involvement. Instead, they sought to present a measured account that indicates the promise of home–school knowledge exchange activity, whilst also recognizing the difficulties and complexities involved.

Conclusions

The four initiatives discussed in this chapter exemplify a number of factors that appear to underpin good practice when schools reach out to engage with parents who might be described as hard to reach. Griffiths' work with *The Letterbox Club* represents a highly inventive response to the needs of children in care, aiming to improve their literacy and numeracy. There was a very clear focus on providing children with learning materials, and these were conveyed to the children in an imaginative, engaging manner. The perspectives of foster parents were respected and played a part in how this project was conducted. A feature of the *Drop in for Coffee* scheme that stands out is the successful strategy used for recruiting parents. The carefully thought-through informality of the approach adopted in this project appeared to avoid a typical danger of such initiatives – stigmatizing parents who participate. The simplicity of the INSPIRE framework for involving parents means that it is adaptable and can probably be used in a range of differing contexts, meeting the needs of a variety of parent and family groups. Finally, the core message from the HSKE project is that variety is important when designing strategies for engaging so-called hard to reach parents – diverse approaches may need to be considered in order to meet the needs of different groups.

In the next chapter, there is a change of focus, and we explore UK-based home visiting as a means of engaging with parents.

5

The Place of Home Visiting

Introduction

Home visiting as a means of promoting family engagement in children's learning has been adopted in a range of projects. This form of intervention offers opportunities for professionals to work closely with families where it may be advantageous for support to be delivered at home rather than expecting families to attend school- or centre-based events.

Clearly, it is vital that the relationships between families and those conducting home visits are built on professionals' awareness that parents play an essential and pivotal role in supporting children's development. This chapter starts with a discussion of conceptualizations of professional–parent relationships that reflect differing levels of such awareness. Then, two UK early intervention projects are discussed (both of which were conducted by researchers at the University of Bristol, and were based in homes and schools located in the city of Bristol): the Literacy Early Action Project, a home-visiting project designed to help young children with literacy difficulties by establishing links between schools and parents, and the South West Autism

Engaging 'Hard to Reach' Parents: Teacher–Parent Collaboration to Promote Children's Learning By Anthony Feiler © 2010 John Wiley & Sons, Ltd

Project, a scheme for families with young children with autistic spectrum disorders. Finally, there is a commentary on issues that are common across both these studies, with discussion of implications for practice. It should be noted that although neither study specifically targeted 'hard to reach parents', home visiting may enhance the development of effective collaboration with parents who, for a variety of reasons, might experience difficulties engaging with schools or with professionals from social care agencies, and for this reason they form the focus for this chapter.

Background

When professionals visit families at home and work closely with parents, it is important that the relationships that develop lead to a respectful and trusting collaboration. In his seminal article 'The professional-lay relationship: a Victorian legacy', Midwinter (1977) eloquently describes the gulf that used to exist between professionals and parents. Midwinter argues that in the past professionals were inclined to adhere rigidly to an outmoded Victorian framework, approaching their roles with an air of dispensing 'charity'. This had the unfortunate consequence of distancing professionals from those with whom they worked, casting professionals in the role of aloof experts. Cunningham and Davis (1985, discussed in Frederickson and Cline, 2002) explore the relationship between professionals and parents of children with special educational needs and consider three models that are implicit in the way that professionals interact with parents: the expert model (which accords with Midwinter's characterization of Victorian professionals' relationships with parents), the transplant model and the consumer model:

- **Expert model.** Professionals whose approach is characterized by this way of working tend to consider that their expertise and knowledge are superior to that of parents. A low priority is given to the views of parents and children, and professionals tend to take the lead in making decisions about intervention. Parents' confidence in their ability to support their child may be undermined, and this may lead to a degree of dependence on professional advice.

- **Transplant model.** As with the expert model, professionals view their own expertise as paramount, but they acknowledge that parents may become a useful source of help through a process of skills being transplanted into parents. There may be a need to enhance parents' skills, but decision-making about teaching and intervention is retained by professionals. As professionals rely on parents to give support at home and provide feedback on the child's progress, parents' self-confidence is likely to be enhanced and professionals are more likely to take a holistic view of the child (recognizing the importance of taking account of family and social factors that might impact on the child's development).
- **Consumer model.** Practitioners whose approach reflects this model regard parents not as passive recipients of professional expertise but as consumers of their services. It is recognized that parents have the right to select which services and which aspects of services might be relevant for their child and for their family circumstances. Decision-making is the prerogative of parents, and the parent–professional relationship is characterized by flexibility and negotiation.

Cunningham and Davis emphasize that in practice professionals' relationships with parents may well reflect aspects of all three models; nevertheless, their analysis provides a useful framework for characterizing this complex process. It is worth noting that features of the consumer model chime with Williamson et al.'s (2006) account of professionals in New Zealand valuing parents' contribution to the assessment process, discussed in Chapter 3.

An influential UK scheme that entails a home-visiting element has been developed by Peter Hannon, Cathy Nutbrown and other researchers at the University of Sheffield. The *Raising Early Achievement in Literacy* (REAL) project is a family literacy programme that aims to promote the literacy development of pre-school children, particularly children who are likely to experience difficulties (Nutbrown et al., 2005). The researchers devised a framework for capturing key parental roles. In order to develop early literacy skills, Nutbrown et al. suggest that parents need to provide Opportunities, Recognition, Interaction and Modelling (ORIM), and children need exposure to certain crucial early literacy experiences (e.g. access to picture books and environmental print such as street names). The ORIM framework is presented in Table 5.1.

Table 5.1   The ORIM framework (based on Nutbrown et al., 2005).

		Important early literacy experiences			
		Environmental print	*Books*	*Early writing*	*Oral language*
Key experiences provided by parents	*Opportunities* (e.g. providing materials for children's drawing and writing)				
	Recognition (e.g. showing/ displaying children's drawing or writing)				
	Interaction (e.g. playing word games)				
	Model (e.g. reading a newspaper or TV guide)				

Portage is another outstanding initiative. It is one of the longest established home-visiting services for children with learning difficulties in the United Kingdom and places a great value on parents' knowledge and expertise. This home-visiting service was originally developed in America, and the first scheme in the United Kingdom was developed during the 1970s. The UK's National Portage Association (www.portage.org.uk) describes the Portage scheme as a home-visiting educational service for pre-school children with additional support needs and their families. Parents are offered weekly home visits (lasting approximately 1 hour) by a trained Portage home visitor. Developmental checklists and parental knowledge help with the process of identifying children's strengths and deciding on future learning goals; there is an emphasis on finding out what a child can already do and then building on this. Parents take the lead in planning learning goals and ensuring that the support offered by Portage home visitors is relevant to the needs of their child and to the needs of the family. During weekly home visits, the Portage home visitor typically asks about the progress made by the child since the previous session, and plans activities jointly with parents that will help the child achieve success during the coming week. Each new skill acquired by the child is usually a step towards a longer term goal and parents often record the child's progress on a chart provided by the home visitor. A 'consumer model' characterizes the relationship between the home visitor and parents that is promoted by the Portage scheme, and interventions are individualized and match the needs of the child and the family: 'Portage offers a framework of support which respects each family and their own individual priorities. It is a model that adapts flexibly to individual child and family needs' (www.portage.org.uk).

The principal strength of the Portage model is the provision of relatively intense, practical support offered to families with young children with learning and other developmental difficulties. Research on the needs of parents with young disabled children consistently points to parents' wishes for early, practical guidance on challenges such as how to develop their child's communication skills and how to manage their child's behaviour. The Portage model provides a framework that can address such issues and is highly valued by parents – it provides a flexible framework that is both structured and supportive, and places the parent at the centre of decision-making.

In the following section, there is discussion of a home-visiting project aimed at supporting young children's early literacy development, where parents play a central role in supporting their child and which includes elements similar to those of the Portage model.

The Literacy Early Action Project

This part of the chapter is taken from early intervention research involving home visiting, conducted by the author and Elaine Logan (Feiler and Logan, 2007). We present a case study of a child who made strong progress with literacy during his first year at a school in Bristol when he participated in the Literacy Early Action Project, and explore factors that contributed to this outcome. During this literacy early intervention project, teaching assistants made weekly home visits and developed literacy support activities with parents/carers for Reception children who were judged by their teachers to be at risk of struggling with literacy.

A rationale for developing close links between schools and parents of young children is the increasing acceptance of the finding that home provides a highly significant foundation for later learning, and literacy practices at home are contributory factors in children's success or failure at school (Gregory and Williams, 2004). Cairney (2003) has pointed out that although researchers have long emphasized the importance of early home learning, it has only relatively recently been recognized that the influence of family members extends beyond the point at which children start school. One approach that schools can consider for building closer links between schools and parents is home visiting, which can be an effective mechanism for offering support to parents in the familiar surroundings of their home.

Increasing the number of teaching assistants and involving them more directly in literacy teaching has been an important element of the strategy in the United Kingdom to raise literacy standards in primary schools and to facilitate the development of more individualized approaches and small-group work. However, a UK government report notes that teaching assistants do not always have sufficient confidence and knowledge to develop literacy intervention programmes (Office for Standards in Education, 2004). Furthermore, there is little research in the United Kingdom on exploring the role that teaching assistants can play in facilitating parental involvement. This account of the Literacy Early Action Project presents a framework within which a teaching assistant successfully applied her knowledge about literacy learning to support a young child and his family with literacy development. Schools can consider this framework when creating opportunities for teaching assistants to work closely with parents in order to support young children's learning.

The Literacy Early Action Project: action taken

The Literacy Early Action Project is an early intervention scheme providing home-based support for parents of Reception children (i.e. children aged 4–5 years, in their first year of statutory schooling) judged by their teachers to be in need of additional help with literacy. During the first half of the Autumn term, Reception teachers and teaching assistants identify two children per class who, they anticipate, may experience difficulties with literacy learning. Following a training event, a teaching assistant (preferably based in the Reception class) visits the families of two children on a weekly basis (visits last approximately 1 hour). Home visiting generally starts during the second half of the Autumn term.

This account of an individual child and his family draws on data that were collected during a project involving four inner-city schools where eight children were identified for additional support. Home visiting for most of the children started in November 2003 and continued until June 2004. Each school was allocated £400 for the purchase of literacy materials for use by the children and their families. Elaine Logan was appointed as a part-time researcher for this project, and she provided support during weekly team meetings for the four teaching assistants who conducted the home visits. Quantitative data on the progress made by the eight children in the four schools indicated that they gained new literacy skills during the year and that their literacy-gain trajectories were generally in line with those of the other children in the Reception classes. However, one of the project children, Yousef, made considerable gains when compared with other children in his class. The main focus of this account of the home-visiting project will be an exploration of factors linked to Yousef's literacy gains.

Yousef attended Cook Primary school (the names of the case study child and the project school have been changed), which was described in an inspection report as a smaller than average school serving an extremely disadvantaged inner-city area. Over 70% of the pupils spoke English as an additional language, with a similar proportion entitled to free school meals (more than three times the national average). Pupil mobility was very high, with large numbers of children leaving and joining throughout the school year. Children's attainment at the time of joining the school was markedly low, especially with regard to literacy and social skills. Despite the very considerable challenges facing staff at this school, the quality of education was judged to be good, and it was noted that the teachers had been very successful in creating a positive learning atmosphere in each class. The leadership and management of the head teacher were singled out for praise. The head teacher's vision, determination and wholehearted commitment were judged to be at the centre of the improvements made at the school in recent years, and it was noted that parents had great confidence in her and her staff.

At the time of this study, Yousef (an only child who spoke English as a first language) and his mother were living with his two cousins aged 8 and 11 years in Yousef's grandparents' house, after a fire destroyed much of their home. Yousef's mother had part-time, manual employment in the evenings. Before the project started, Yousef had been placed on the school's special educational needs register because of concerns about his behaviour. The Reception teacher chose Yousef to participate in this study because she anticipated that his involvement would enhance his approach to learning: 'He doesn't really have the social skills to access his learning and I thought it [the Literacy Early Action Project] would help him to focus and concentrate more.'

During the Reception year, the teaching assistant (who was based in the Reception class) made 26 visits to Yousef's home. This number was relatively high – in comparison with an average of 16 home visits for the other seven project children where regular home visiting was maintained. Yousef's mother was employed during the week as a cleaner from 4.30 to 6.30 p.m. and was not always at home when the teaching assistant made her weekly visits. So on these occasions, the teaching assistant met with Yousef's grandparents and they played a prominent role in encouraging Yousef to engage with the literacy activities that had been discussed. Examples of literacy activities devised for Yousef are given in Box 5.1.

Box 5.1   Examples of literacy activities devised for Yousef during the Literacy Early Action Project.

November 2003. Mother/grandparents to read short stories and Yousef to retell in his own words; play matching game with cards (matching letter sounds to pictures of objects that start with the same sound); learn to name and sound three letters.

January 2004. Use matching cards to recognize keywords from the *Oxford Reading Tree* series: mum, dad, Biff, Chip, Kipper. Practise writing first name; learn to name and sound five letters.

March 2004. Play wordsearch game (Yousef to identify 12 keywords embedded in a two-dimensional grid); reading and writing 12 keywords; playing Bingo game with keywords (players match word-cards with keywords on a board); draw lines to join pictures of animals to their names.

June 2004. Yousef to read from story book; write giant words outside in garden with large chalks; invent single-syllable words that rhyme and record these in a book with help from his mother.

Note. Although some of the examples above reflect a playful approach to learning (e.g. introducing matching and Bingo games), there was also focus on what might be termed more 'traditional' aspects of literacy learning such as naming and sounding letters and identifying individual words on cards.

In Cook Primary school, all the children in the Reception class (including Yousef) were tested using the Performance Indicators in Primary Schools (PIPS) materials (PIPS Project, 2002). Baseline assessments were conducted in October 2003 and outcome data were collected in June/July 2004. In addition to the PIPS assessment, interviews were conducted with Yousef's mother, the teaching assistant who conducted the home visits, the Reception teacher and the head teacher. Two group interviews were held with the teaching assistants who participated in the project.

Yousef's literacy progress

During the baseline assessment, which was conducted at the start of the Reception year, Yousef used letter-like marks when attempting to write his name. However, when shown individual letters from the alphabet he was unable to give names or sounds for any of these, and he could not identify/read single words. When assessed at the end of the Reception year, Yousef had made much progress. When asked to write his name, all the letters were recognizable, he was able to give names or sounds for 25 of the 26 letters, and he was also able to identify 10 common words (such as house, duck, dog and cat).

Yousef's baseline reading score on the PIPS test (PIPS Project, 2002), before the home visiting started, placed him on rank 13 in the class of 17 students. By the end of the Reception year, Yousef's reading score on the PIPS test resulted in a gain of 9 positions (compared to

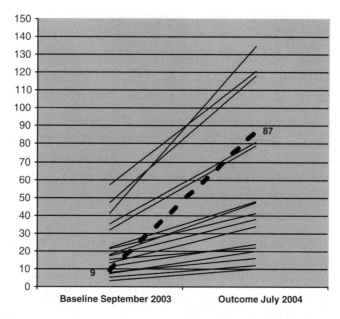

Figure 5.1   Baseline and outcome reading raw scores (PIPS) for Cook Primary Reception class (Yousef's trajectory is marked with a broken line).

how he performed at the start of the year) and he reached rank 4. Yousef's reading performance on this test was equivalent to the national average for Reception children. Figure 5.1 shows the gains in reading raw scores on the PIPS test made by Yousef and other children in his class during the Reception year.

In the next section, we present the core themes that emerged from semi-structured interviews conducted with Yousef's mother, the teaching assistant, Reception class teacher and head teacher. The selection of these themes reflects the main focus of this case study – to explore factors that were linked to Yousef's gains with literacy.

The teaching assistant's sensitivity to family culture

The first theme reflects the warmth and ease that characterized the teaching assistant's approach to family involvement when home visits were conducted. Her respect for parents and her proactive approach while working with them appeared to underpin the successful relationship she developed with Yousef's mother and grandparents:

RESEARCH QUOTATION

'. . . I like being with the parents. I think sometimes – some schools, some teachers or teaching assistants – they treat the parents as outsiders or inferior, or give them that kind of impression . . . I think if you've got a good relationship with the parents, it's going to make teaching their children a lot easier. And if you can approach them at every level and don't allow things to build up – if something happens, say, "This thing happened today". If you say, "Last week he did this", parents get very upset about that. We must talk to them every day – well, as often as we see them. Get to understand each other, get to know each other on their level, not talk down to them.'

Teaching assistant from the Literacy Early Action Project

The importance of professionals' sensitivity to family culture has been strongly emphasized in the literature on early intervention. Dyson and Robson (1999) observe that it is imperative for intervention programmes to respect and build on what parents are already doing and avoid forms of 'cultural imperialism'. Edwards and Warin (1999) are similarly concerned that hard-pressed primary school teachers working with an overloaded curriculum may be tempted to view parents merely as a source of additional pedagogic assistance and warn that collaboration can easily become colonization. These authors argue convincingly for the need for the joint construction of parental roles in order to create reciprocally acceptable sets of expectations.

Flexibility that facilitates involvement of extended family members

A significant feature of the Literacy Early Action Project was the degree to which a wide range of family members, siblings and friends of the child typically became involved at home in the literacy activities, and an important factor underpinning the home-visiting process was flexibility shown by the teaching assistants. This included negotiating visiting times that suited the family and suggesting activities with which other family members could become involved, including younger siblings and grandparents (Feiler, 2005). In the present study, Yousef's grandparents played a significant role in his care, helping to look after him when his mother worked. So it was important that a relationship developed that enabled Yousef's grandparents and other family members to engage in the process of supporting his literacy learning. This was recognized by the teaching assistant, and it emerged that Yousef's cousins (who lived with Yousef at the same address) also participated in the literacy activities. Yousef's mother commented: 'Yes they do, they poke their nose in sometimes! [i.e. Yousef's cousins joining in with the literacy activities] ... they do it with him because sometimes I don't have the time. So I ask his older cousin to help him with it, so she's sort of involved in that way. If I don't have the time, she'll fill in for me.'

Putting the child at the centre of the intervention

It was evident from the comments made by Yousef's mother and teaching assistant that Yousef enjoyed the home visits: 'He was excited [about the Literacy Early Action Project visits] ... At first he was tired after school. But now he knows that on Wednesdays, X [teaching assistant] will come and he looks forward to it and is not tired anymore ... he keeps reminding me that it's Wednesday, so he knows when she's coming.' Furthermore, it is likely that Yousef's enjoyment of the home-based sessions reflected the teaching assistant's emphasis on placing Yousef at the centre of the intervention. Yousef's teaching assistant described her approach: 'I said to him [Yousef], "What are we going to do this evening?" when I get there, "What are we going to do?" and we go on from there. I slip my own little bit in that I've got planned, or if that's not working just follow their lead.'

Viewing children as the focal point for parent–teacher involvement approaches has been recognized by researchers on the Home–School Knowledge Exchange Project, discussed in the previous chapter (Feiler et al., 2007). It has been found that children are often the best ambassadors for new initiatives, and putting the child at the centre of activities where schools and parents work together can result in very positive outcomes for children's literacy learning.

Using a playful approach

Commentary from the teaching assistant highlighted the extent to which she believed that using a playful approach was an important factor in facilitating young children's learning: '[I] get on the floor and play. You can teach a child anything just playing, and they don't realise that they are learning. A friend said to me, "I don't know how you do it" – whenever she came to my house I was on the floor with my children.'

There is support in the research literature for a link between play and the sound development of early literacy skills. Roskos and Chistie (2001) have reviewed studies conducted during the 1990s on the relationship between play and early literacy and conclude that there is strong evidence that play contributes to children's literacy development. In a similar vein, Marsh and Millard (2000) suggest that playful approaches not only enhance young children's confidence with literacy learning but can also provide a natural link between home and school.

School cultures that promote parental involvement

It should be noted that the focus on parental involvement was central to staff values at Cook Primary school. The head teacher had built strong links with parents in the community and was respected by local families, and the Literacy Early Action Project was viewed as a natural extension to the work the school was already undertaking with parents. Similarly, the Reception teacher's emphasis on ensuring that parents had ready access to her when they brought their children to school and collected them at the end of the day was another indicator of the school's determination to develop effective links with parents.

The Literacy Early Action Project: discussion of findings

The progress made by the case study child during the Literacy Early Action Project was substantial. Despite weak literacy skills at the start of school, by the end of the year Yousef's development gave him one of the strongest literacy profiles in his Reception class. It is probable that the home-visiting support offered by the teaching assistant played a significant role, for it is apparent from other home-visiting initiatives that modelling approaches for parents in home settings tends to be an effective strategy for family involvement. Yousef's mother, grandparents and cousins became actively engaged in his early literacy development and it is likely that the teaching assistant's flexible approach with the family facilitated this process. This, together with the other key factors that emerged (the teaching assistant's sensitivity to family culture, the playful approach to learning she adopted, putting the child at the centre of the intervention and the existence of a school culture that strongly promoted parental involvement), appears to have contributed to Yousef's literacy learning. These aspects contributed to the quality of support Yousef received from his mother and grandparents; this links with the increasingly convincing evidence that one of the strongest predictors of young children's literacy development is support for literacy at home (National Literacy Trust, 2005).

The outcomes of this case study are in line with the findings reported by Sylva et al. (2004) from the Effective Provision of Pre-School Education (EPPE) project, a major European longitudinal study of a national sample of young children's development between the ages of 3 and 7 years. When discussing children's learning, Sylva et al. emphasize the importance of a home environment where parents are actively engaged in activities with children, as this promotes intellectual and social development. The authors also note that although parents' social class and level of education were linked to children's learning outcomes in the EPPE project, the quality of the home learning environment was found to be more important, and it was established that what parents did with their children was more important than parental social background factors.

It is notable that in the Literacy Early Action Project the teaching assistant openly valued the contribution made by the family to Yousef's developing literacy skills, actively acknowledging that their contribution mattered. Rather than holding a deficit view of Yousef and his family – viewing them as being 'needy' because they lacked certain skills or values – she believed in building on the family's social capital, working with different family members to enhance Yousef's development. This reflects aspects of a sociocultural perspective on learning, where it is recognized that children's development cannot be isolated from the contexts in which it occurs, and where engagement with children in an authentic setting (the home) leads us to embrace the conditions and environments which children experience, however unpredictable or complex they may be.

The fact that the teaching assistant worked in the Reception class at Yousef's school and made regular visits to the home signifies that she was very well placed to discuss literacy activities that corresponded closely with Yousef's specific attainment levels and were carefully matched to the resources and support available in the family environment. This reflects a finding reported by inspectors from the Office for Standards in Education (Office for Standards in Education, 2004), who explored parental involvement and found that schools that were more effective in supporting literacy learning tended to encourage parents' specific engagement in literacy. The potential contribution made by teaching assistants to children's learning is being increasingly recognized. A report by government inspectors notes: 'In the best cases, teachers involve teaching assistants in planning for pupils or, at the very least, ensure that they are briefed fully' (Office for Standards in Education, 2005, p. 22). A principal implication of the Literacy Early Action Project is that teaching assistants in the United Kingdom might be given more scope to develop not only support strategies for young children but also approaches that involve collaborative work with parents.

The South West Autism Project is another early intervention research project that explores the use of home-based support for parents.

The South West Autism Project

In this section, selected findings are presented from a research study involving parents of children with autistic spectrum disorders (Webster et al., 2004). As with children who experience literacy difficulties, the field of autism is another area where home-based intervention for young children can be highly valued by parents.

The South West Autism Project (SWAP) used a home-visiting framework to provide early intervention support for parents of young children diagnosed with autistic spectrum disorders in the Bristol area. Home-visiting tutors paid particular attention to the families' circumstances and preferences, including existing patterns of communication and social interaction between family members. Good practice in designing and implementing services involves putting children and families first and adapting intervention to the existing competencies and routines in families – not vice versa. This has been termed being sensitive to the 'ecology of the particular child and family' (McCollum, 2002, p. 6). In a review of early intervention research, McCollum identifies a significant guiding principle that children's development cannot be separated from the contexts in which it occurs. As with the approach adopted in the Literacy Early Action Project, it follows that intervention should not be solely treatment-focused or child-focused, but should also take into account the parental, sibling or childcare environments that influence the developmental opportunities available to the child. The principle of 'development-in-context' leads to forms of intervention that strengthen (rather than replace) the capacity of family members to respond to and engage with your children as a foundation for social interaction, language and cognitive growth.

The main focus of the research discussed here is on exploring the views of parents of children with autistic spectrum disorders (ASDs). Parents' views were sought on issues that included not only their experiences of home-visiting support and aspects of early intervention that were particularly valued, but also their experience of initial diagnostic procedures and the impact of having a child with an ASD on family life. The sample of parents included six families who were managing their own intervention. Prior to the setting up of SWAP, a number of families had requested and been awarded funding by the Local Authority to manage their own intensive interventions on the basis of applied behavioural analysis (ABA), in a context where there was no dedicated pre-school provision for children with ASDs. Typically, these families were advised by ABA consultants external to the Local Authority, who made initial assessments of children, advised on treatment plans and made periodic reviews of children's progress. In most versions of ABA, new skills are taught in a series of drills where target behaviours are worked on (such as following a command to sit down, draw a shape or look at an adult's face), with correct responses rewarded by praise, tokens or food. Behaviour that is judged to be inappropriate or unwanted, such as rocking or hand flapping, tends to be ignored. ABA tutors work directly with children and involve parents in implementation, which may come to 40 hours training for each child per week for 2 years or more.

In contrast, SWAP was eclectic in orientation. Nine families agreed to participate in the research and received help from SWAP family tutors trained in behavioural approaches, encompassing methods from speech therapy, such as intensive interaction and the Picture Exchange Communication System (PECS), and other strategies such as visual timetables and the use of social scripts. There was a strong emphasis on adopting flexible approaches that could be tailored to families' needs: for example, a child with little eye contact and poor social skills was taught turn-taking and how to make requests using a bubble-blowing game; a child who withdrew into a trance-like state, even on short-distance car journeys, was given an 'I-spy' card to help him keep alert; and a child who had difficulties accepting change was presented with a 'surprise' card to help him anticipate a change in routine.

Parents negotiated contact hours with the family tutor, up to a maximum of 25 hours per week, and the arrangement was reviewed at least every 3 months. The agreed time averaged 10 hours per week per family (ranging from 2.5 to 25 hours per week). It is worth noting that families varied markedly in their expressed preferences for intervention, with the majority of parents requesting a mixture of strategies that were custom-made to suit their children's needs, rather than a pure ABA-style approach. Families also varied widely in the active roles they took in working directly with their own children and in the degree to which they were able to generate elements of the programme for themselves. In most cases, however, parents contributed to delivering and practising aspects of the programme beyond the contact time from SWAP family tutors. Much of the work was geared to enabling children to develop active spontaneous intentional communication and engagement with communication partners, identified as a key factor in tackling ASDs (Potter and Whittaker, 2001).

Regular home visiting allowed the SWAP tutors to hand over strategies to parents and siblings, modelling and coaching their use, and the longer term aim was to enhance the communication environment in the family and to empower the family to act independently and autonomously. Another element of SWAP was that tutors also worked closely with staff in pre-school settings to facilitate smooth transitions between home and playgroup, nursery or school. This involved tutors shadowing children into mainstream, handing over strategies that had worked well with individual children at home and problem-solving when any barriers arose in group settings. Children were also equipped, as far as possible, with the social skills to join in with other children and groups, understand instructions and cope with the routines of the school day.

It was decided that a rich picture of parental views should be sought, using questionnaires and semi-structured interviews as key research tools. The views of 15 families with children with ASDs were explored: 10 families receiving SWAP intervention at the time this research was conducted were approached, and 9 agreed to be interviewed; 7 families using self-managed ABA methods were also contacted, and 6 families agreed to participate in the research (thus, a total of 15 families agreed to be contacted and interviewed). The age range of the children was from 2 years and 9 months to 6 years and 8 months. Although some interviews were conducted with both parents present, most respondents were mothers. All of the direct quotes below are taken from interviews with the nine mothers who were receiving support from SWAP family tutors.

The South West Autism Project – key findings

Priorities for practical help

A strong theme to emerge (mentioned by 9 of the 15 parents) was the lack of information about practical help immediately following the ASD diagnosis. Professionals were typically viewed by parents as insensitive to the needs of families, many of whom appeared to see their role as not extending beyond diagnosis:

> **RESEARCH QUOTATION**
>
> '. . . *from the October and the November* [period immediately following diagnosis] *I made over two hundred phone calls – I'm not exaggerating, you should see my phone bill. I phoned everyone and everything to do with autism . . . I wanted help and I wanted help straight away.*'
>
> '. . . *we just sat in a room. "OK she's got autism. Let's have a look at her. Right, I'll see you in six months time" . . . You've got the diagnosis, and you're stuck . . . not even to be pointed in any sort of direction just was really scary, really scary.*'
>
> **Mothers from the South West Autism Project**

Parents were asked about the period between receiving a diagnosis and the start of intervention from SWAP or ABA tutors, and they were asked about which aspects of their child's development they most wanted advice from professionals. The two issues that dominated this area (identified by 13 out of the 15 parents) were children's communication/language skills and behaviour. It was apparent from the strength of views expressed that parental concerns about managing their child's potentially difficult behaviour, particularly in public places, led to considerable stress.

Families' isolation

A strong theme in both questionnaire responses and interviews was the profound impact of ASDs: all but one of the parents felt that their child's needs had altered their family life. This manifested itself in a number of ways. Most (10 out of 15 parents) found that they had to reduce work commitments to meet their child's needs. Furthermore, there was substantial commentary on the extent to which their child's needs had resulted in some degree of isolation and a reduction of contact with other families and friends, and the manner in which their relationship with other children in the family had been affected:

RESEARCH QUOTATION

'. . . we've also found that a lot of what used to be friends, as soon as she was diagnosed, we seemed to find out who our real friends were. They all seemed to wither away like it was some sort of disease . . . They just disappeared. I haven't got time for them [other children in the family]. I'm always tired a lot of the time. And it's not necessarily being able to chase around, it's mentally as well. I've got the disability forms to fill out, like the blue badge I need to chase up. That sort of thing, and it's constant, the worrying'

(Mother from the South West Autism Project)

Aspects of intervention particularly valued

When parents were asked to identify aspects of the intervention approach they most valued, 'help with communication' came up strongly (mentioned by 10 of the 15 families). Some parents emphasized how their child's developing language and communication skills helped with integration within the family:

RESEARCH QUOTATION

'Yes, increasing X's desire to communicate, not just increasing his communication, but his desire to be part of the family. That's what's really taken it to the next level for us really. Losing the desire for him to be on his own the whole time really. He's definitely started to interact with us all more really, just being part of the family. I think I would, you know, say that SWAP has made a massive difference.'

Mother from the South West Autism Project

Parents' comments on behaviour management underlined their appreciation of help with specific aspects of their child's behaviour:

RESEARCH QUOTATION

'With the sleeping I could have seen X [health service specialist] but it was really hard to get to see him about her sleeping habits. But they [SWAP tutors] gave me some ideas. She's not brilliant, but I can get her to bed now. But that's what I mean, things like that. They [tutors] don't have to do that . . . they could just walk away from that. Instead you just feel that they get really involved in your life.'

Mother from the South West Autism Project

Flexibility was another important issue to emerge in what parents valued about the support offered by family tutors. For example, one mother commented: 'They listen to what the parents need, rather than, as I said, coming in with a set course.'

Transition points

One of the concerns raised by many parents related to apprehensions about their child transferring from home to a mainstream setting, or from a nursery to a school setting. Although home-based intervention from tutors probably eased children's transition, a number of families anticipated that this might be a difficult hurdle to negotiate: 'I'm just frightened to death for her. It's just such a big step for her, because she's been in this cosy little nursery, that have all, not tiptoed round her, but all the children are so young. And they just see X as being X and that she's not different. But already we're getting kids over there –

there's one who keeps grabbing her, a little boy – bullying and things like that. Because she wouldn't know how to defend herself.'

The South West Autism Project: discussion and implications for practice

A common concern voiced by most parents in this study relates to initial delays: first, in having their concerns taken seriously, and second, the time taken to provide practical advice and intervention following the point at which an ASDs diagnosis is formalized. There is general consensus in the literature on children with disabilities that early diagnosis is important in order that appropriate intervention such as the home-visiting support can be implemented as soon as possible (Charman and Baird, 2002). However, although there has been a general decrease in the age of children at which autism is confirmed, this has not necessarily been matched by the provision of appropriate services.

Bringing up children with disabilities can be immensely demanding, and some of the stressors specific to ASDs are reflected in the way parents prioritize practical advice and help. These include dealing with children's obsessions, achieving sleep patterns and routines for toileting, establishing functional communication and managing difficult behaviour in public such as tantrums in shops and running away, exacerbated by the 'normal' appearance of children. These issues are echoed in the demands made by parents for intervention approaches that are flexible, realistic and relevant to the families' own concerns and knowledge of their children. Intervention that is offered within a home-visiting framework enables tutors to take account of and respond to families' diverse needs, and to be sensitive to family-specific opportunities and constraints. The principle of 'development-in-context' mentioned earlier emphasizes the importance of individualizing services, of taking close account of family needs and circumstances and of strengthening the capacity of parents to generate appropriate intervention strategies for themselves, beyond any direct inputs provided from outside.

For most parents, the transition from home to school and from a pre-school setting to a mainstream context can be an anxious time, and for children with ASDs who are often resistant to changes in routine, these transitions may be extremely demanding and difficult to manage. It is vital that services offered to families with young children with ASDs are sufficiently flexible to allow professionals to prepare the ground thoroughly when transitions are anticipated, helping to bridge the gap between one context and another. Workers who have been able to establish a relationship with children and parents during a period of home visiting will be soundly positioned to support this process. Bringing up a pre-school child with a disability is a potentially stressful experience that may have a profound impact on the family's functioning. As discussed in Chapter 1, one of the implications of sociocultural theory is that parents are more likely to manage difficulties effectively when their reserves of social capital are high and connections with other groups are in place. It was apparent that a number of parents in this project experienced social isolation from family and friends as a result of having a child with autism, and this seemed to undermine their capacity to cope.

Conclusions

Although the Literacy Early Action Project and the South West Autism Project offered support to families with young children with very different needs, both schemes used home visiting as a key method of service delivery. In this final section, issues common to both projects are considered.

Sensitivity to family customs and conduct

In both studies, the teaching assistants and family tutors explicitly valued and built on current family practices and what parents were already doing, and avoided imposing their own values on families. In SWAP this was referred to as the principle of 'development-in-context', which emphasized the importance of individualizing services and paying close attention to family needs and circumstances.

Flexibility and the importance of facilitating the involvement of extended family members

It became apparent to those conducting home visits that a range of family members, family friends and siblings of the target child needed to be involved in the activities and approaches that were discussed. In order to embrace diverse family contexts, a key factor that underpinned the development of successful relationships with families involved the home visitor adopting a flexible approach – for example negotiating visiting times that suited parents and developing activities with which other family members could engage.

Putting children and families first

Placing children and families at the heart of a support programme involved adapting interventions to the existing competencies and child-rearing practices in families. Activities that suited the needs of children and families were developed, rather than imposing a pre-determined curriculum. At the start of this chapter, there is discussion of Cunningham and Davis' (1985) examination of the way that professionals relate to parents of children with special educational needs. They suggest that there are dangers of professionals assuming the role of the expert, and argue instead that professionals need to adopt an approach where there is shared decision-making during which negotiation and flexibility underpin the parent–professional relationship. There were indications that these features were present in the Literacy Early Action Project and SWAP. It is likely that the presence of these features was due in part to a home-visiting framework that allowed teaching assistants and tutors to get to know families over time, to devise support strategies that put the child's and families' needs first and to develop a 'joint construction of expertise' (McNaughton, 2001) where parental and professional expertise was shared.

6

Caveats and Concerns

Introduction

This chapter considers the challenges and problems that can arise when schools work closely with parents who may have difficulties engaging with schools. An important theme raised earlier in the book and revisited here relates to the language used to describe marginalized groups and the inherent danger of certain terminology implying that some families have deficits or are in some way inferior to other families. Another problematic aspect considered in this chapter is the assumption that parents necessarily welcome close contacts with schools. Some parents hold strong views about involvement and may actively challenge the expectation that this is part of their role. Furthermore, some children and young people may have reservations about the extent to which their parents engage with education and schooling. There is also discussion of the assumptions that are sometimes developed by professionals working with disabled children and their parents. The chapter concludes with commentary on concerns that certain aspects of the research literature on home–school links can be rather superficial.

Engaging 'Hard to Reach' Parents: Teacher–Parent Collaboration to Promote Children's Learning By Anthony Feiler © 2010 John Wiley & Sons, Ltd

Some of the commentary in this chapter has been taken from Feiler et al.'s (2006) article on the Home–School Knowledge Exchange project.

Hard to reach parents – problems with terminology

The phrase 'hard to reach' has been used extensively in recent years, and the notion that professionals find it difficult to make connections with some groups is widespread across policy areas. Coined originally by research agencies such as MORI (Market and Opinion Research International) to indicate that traditional research methods were inappropriate for some groups, the expression 'hard to reach' has come broadly to denote groups who do not access services or engage with provision, and may be used interchangeably with the term 'socially excluded' (Milbourne, 2002). Within the literature on social exclusion, the use of the term 'hard to reach' is starting to be problematized, and one of the principal concerns is its lack of clarity. The range of those described as 'hard to reach' by government and service providers is wide and can include minority ethnic groups, the 'overlooked' (such as the learning disabled) and those who might be described as disaffected (Doherty et al., 2004). Rather than being a precise term with a commonly agreed definition, there is a danger that the expression 'hard to reach' is an expedient catch-all phrase that merely signals difficulties encountered by professionals in engaging or making contact with others.

As discussed in Chapter 2, a related concern in this field is the possibility that the expression 'hard to reach' promotes deficit views of families. Broadhurst et al. note: 'Official discourses that centre on generalized characteristics of "problem" populations can … stereotype and stigmatise' (Broadhurst et al., 2005, p.106). Such terminology implies that it is families' lifestyles, aspirations and conduct that distance them from society's institutions, rather than deficits in society (such as the devastating impact of poor housing and unemployment) that cause such marginalization and vulnerability. There is an assumption that if 'hard to reach' families could be encouraged to conform to the values espoused by society and by schools, health services and other establishments, this would enable them to become 'reachable'. The use of the term 'hard to reach parents' may deflect attention away from the responsibility that services (including schools) bear for ensuring that families find them welcoming and 'reachable'. Rather than adopting a deficit model of parental engagement (some parents have problems that make them 'hard to reach'), a social model might be applied (some parents engage less with schools because of barriers created by schools/society) and attention could be focused more on developing supports within school systems to make them more accessible for all families.

Viewing parents as a homogeneous group

Another problem with describing some parents as 'hard to reach' is that such a descriptor may stereotype and gloss over myriad differences among families – differences that are key to the diversity and variety that characterize individuals and families. Crozier and Reay's work addresses the involvement of relatively disempowered groups and these authors voice concern that parents in general, and particularly parents who might be described as marginalized, tend to be viewed as a uniform, unvarying group:

RESEARCH QUOTATION

'... *far too often parents are perceived either as a homogeneous mass or reduced to a simplistic binary between 'the good' and 'the bad' ... both approaches neglect complex differentiations of class, ethnicity and gender; in addition the still powerful impact of the economic is ignored, and cultural influences are often reduced to deficit models of working class and minority ethnic parents.'*

Crozier and Reay, 2005, pp. 155–156

Crozier's (2004) 2-year study of Bangladeshi and Pakistani families in the North East of England (discussed in Chapter 2) was instigated because of a lack of research on parents from these ethnic groups and because of concerns that children from such families might be underachieving at school. Although there can be a tendency within the literature to refer to Asian families collectively, Crozier found that there were some key differences between the Bangladeshi and Pakistani parents' knowledge, such as their grasp of the English education system. The need to avoid generalized assumptions about minority ethnic groups and the importance of recognizing subtle differences that distinguish one group from another are strongly emphasized in Crozier's research. It may also be important to distinguish important dissimilarities **within** certain groups, differences that distinguish one family from another. In the Home–School Knowledge Exchange project (Feiler et al., 2006), it was frequently found that something that suited one family might not suit another. Variations within particular communities act as a reminder that it is not just the heterogeneity of the parent body as a whole which needs to be taken into account. There is also diversity within groups, especially where the categorization of groups is founded on rather general factors like class and ethnicity.

Parental involvement: an unwelcome intrusion?

Another potential problem in the field of parental engagement is whether the emphasis on parents being more involved in their child's education may, at times, result in intrusive pressures on families. In the Home–School Knowledge Exchange project (Feiler et al., 2006), although most parents welcomed opportunities to help their children with school-related activities at home, some parents found this expectation demanding. As discussed in Chapter 4, during an activity aimed at enhancing the flow of information from homes to schools, some of the children were given disposable cameras over summer holidays. They were asked to take photographs of various subjects, some of which involved number work. Although many children and parents enjoyed the activity, some found it challenging and one mother blamed herself for not being able to generate ideas: 'A fortnight went by and we hadn't taken any pictures and I was thinking, "Oh my god, what are we going to take pictures of him doing?" . . . And I was thinking, well, what do other people do? That was the other thing, I was trying to think of what other people did in their houses that involved numbers that I didn't do. I was thinking, I must be missing something here.'

Carvalho (2001) believes that there can be strong tensions in school–home associations – stronger than the relatively mild self-doubt expressed by this mother. Carvalho argues that parent–teacher relations are inherently conflictive in nature and suggests that Waller's (1932) characterization of parents and teachers as 'natural enemies' still holds today. This is partly due to the fact that parents are inexorably concerned with the individual needs of their children, whereas teachers have a professional responsibility for numbers of children. It is suggested that this clash of interests tends to become problematic when there are concerns about children's performance at school and questions are raised about accountability (in terms of whether teachers or parents are more responsible). Crozier holds similar views about the hostility that can typify school–home relations:

RESEARCH QUOTATION

'Unlike the harmonious, anodyne relationships presented in many of the parental involvement texts, in reality parent–teacher relationships are characterized by a struggle for control and definition. Teachers have two broad sets of relationships to manage: with assertive, demanding middle class parents on the one hand and with the seemingly passive, dis-engaged working class parents on the other.'

Crozier, 2000, p. 123

In a powerful, personal account of her experiences of US schools, Carvalho describes moving with her family from Brazil to the United States. She contrasts her experiences of Brazilian and US schooling and concludes that the pressure placed on parents in the United States to become involved in education is intense. Regardless of whether some parents are unable or unwilling to participate, parents who choose not to become involved are, in her view, seen as negligent by US society. Carvalho argues that the parental involvement move-ment is an intrusion of schooling into family life that subverts how families educate their children in their own ways. She was particu-larly taken aback by the homework demands her children faced in US schools, the teachers' assumption that parental support would be provided at home and that parents would indeed welcome such opportunities:

RESEARCH QUOTATION

'Coming to the U.S. I thought my kids would attend marvellous, rich, effective, whole-day, public schools and, consequently, would never have homework. Therefore, I was quite surprised when they consistently brought schoolwork home. I was appalled when I had to do my part in a fifth-grade interactive homework during the first middle school transition year, and I was perplexed when my signature on a high school history homework was worth 5 extra credit point. As a parent, I felt constrained to do my part in my children's homework and enjoy it.'

Carvalho, 2001, p. 37

Another of Carvalho's concerns about the pressure on parents to become more involved is the problem of inequity. Carvalho proposes that the current focus on parental involvement in the West reflects an outdated notion of school–community relations that fails to take account of the increasing diversity and complexity that typify families today. She argues that families are very different and have differing, unequal amounts of social and cultural capital, so some families will experience considerable difficulties in responding to invitations to become more engaged. Although educational policy might be aimed at so-called needy families, Carvalho argues that such attempts to target support tend to be undermined by powerful socioeconomic factors such as poverty and low educational achievement, and that families with limited resources are unlikely to be able to respond to such educational opportunities. One example is the difficulty that some working parents experience when trying to attend school-based events that clash with working hours. Those in low-paid employment are likely to find it harder to afford time off work to attend such events, or indeed to be allowed such flexibility.

Reay (2005) makes a similar point about parental involvement and the lack of a level playing field. She argues that parents' individual histories and educational experiences influence how effective they are in developing contacts with teachers, and that differences in such capacity are underpinned by social class and ethnicity. The implication is that white, middle-class parents will tend to be more successful when negotiating such contacts than other groups. If Carvalho's and Reay's analysis is accurate, then there is a danger that parental involvement policies may widen the gap between the engagement of more and less affluent parents; because an emphasis on parental involvement may result in families with more resources (financial, social, educational and so forth) being better positioned to gain further advantages in comparison with other families. This might be termed the Matthew effect in parental involvement, that is, the rich getting richer and the poor getting poorer.

What about the views of children on family involvement in education? In the next section, some of the reservations that young people may hold about their parents' involvement are examined.

Children and young people's reservations about family involvement

Children may not always be enthusiastic about their parents becoming involved with schools. As mentioned above, during the Home–School Knowledge Exchange project (Feiler et al., 2006) families used cameras over the summer holidays to take photographs of various activities. One mother felt that her son's lack of interest might have been on account of her own **over** involvement: 'Oh, I remember that one [home–school activity] because he's still got the bleedin' camera . . . I did the activity, he didn't actually use the camera. I don't think he was that, I'm not sure whether he wasn't impressed with it, or he was probably less impressed with the fact that I got involved.' The stepsister of another child thought that she (the child) might have felt too shy to show her pictures at school. The reference to shyness acts as a reminder that children may have different levels of comfort about bringing aspects of the home into school, making the private public. Some children may have concerns about the way their peers might respond to their photographs, or that a discontinuity between their own school identity and their home-based representations would be revealed.

In a study involving secondary-age pupils, Crozier (2000) asked 11–14 year-olds for their perspectives about having to show parents a homework diary and get it signed. Although some welcomed such parental scrutiny, others viewed this as an encroachment on their independence. Furthermore, when Crozier (2004) conducted research with Asian families, she noted the reservations expressed by some pupils regarding the close links their parents developed with schools: '. . . the young people were very independent of their parents with regard to education. In many cases . . . they did not inform their parents of their progress or of school meetings' (Crozier, 2004, p. 9). Crozier found that some of the young people she interviewed were sensitive about comments that might be made during parents' evenings, such as observations about the traditional clothes their parents wore – they wished to shield their parents from such potentially discomforting experiences:

RESEARCH QUOTATION

'[Some Asian pupils] *wanted to protect their parents from embarrassment because of their limited knowledge of English and of the education system. Some pupils also mentioned their concern that their parents might be embarrassed by aspects of the curriculum such as biology. Many felt strongly that the school was not a conducive place for their parents' involvement. Consequently, ironically, they were active in their parents' exclusion.*'

Crozier, 2004, p. 9

When considering factors that influenced students' response to their parents being involved with school, Crozier found that students with weaker academic achievement tended to express less positive responses: 'Not surprisingly, the more disaffected students did not want their parents to know about their lack of "success", or, particularly if they were in any trouble or had failed at a piece of work' (Crozier, 2000, p. 109).

Meeting the needs of parents with disabled children

Another caveat in this field relates to professionals' attitudes towards a particular group of parents – those with a young disabled child. As discussed in Chapter 2, research from international contexts has repeatedly emphasized that the pressures experienced by parents of disabled children can result in increased levels of emotional stress and high rates of breakdown in parental relations. Understandably, professionals working with parents of young disabled children may speculate, when attempting to understand parents' feelings and perspectives, how parents of disabled children react to such pressures. However, sometimes such postulations may be wide of the mark. In an authoritative account, Mallet (1997), who is a parent of two young children with developmental delays, describes a rather overbearing approach used by professionals who were assessing her children's development. In a particularly powerful passage, she critiques a typical assumption that some professionals may adopt. This is the supposition that the emotional reactions of parents with disabled children – such as frustration and fatigue – should be interpreted as parents' reluctance to come to terms with the reality of their child's difficulties, and as a reaction to a sense of loss or grief in not having an able-bodied child. She challenges this viewpoint, suggesting that such a position might reflect over-theorized, defensive professional attitudes:

RESEARCH QUOTATION

'Much has been written about "chronic sorrow" and the so called "grieving process" that parents undergo when they discover that they have failed to produce "the perfect child" ... As a consequence many professionals are taught to interpret exhaustion, confusion, frustration, anger or any other "negativity" from parents, as stages of their coming to terms with a sense of loss associated with their child's "special needs". Having observed that adoptive parents who have had advance knowledge of their child's extra needs (so technically cannot have suffered such loss) seem to react in similar ways to being worn out or let down by people and services that they expected to assist their child, I suspect the origins of much parental discomfort have more to do with poor practice than traumatic disappointment in their child! Applying theory rather than exercising empathy may do more to defend a professional than serve a family.'

Mallett, 1997, p. 29

This sense of disillusionment in the way that professionals sometimes misinterpret parents' reactions was also reflected in the comments from mothers of young children with autistic spectrum disorders during the South West Autism Project (discussed in Chapter 5). Some of the mothers commented that professionals seemed to be unresponsive to families' needs, particularly in relation to the lack of guidance offered on management strategies. One mother commented on her irritation about being asked about her feelings, rather than being offered practical help: 'I was really at my wits' end. X [child] was screaming, biting, I had another child to look after. We used to go to work to get away from it. We had a lot of professional people asking us how we felt. I felt like shit but I wanted to do something, I needed help with X . . . I can sort out my own feelings.'

Accounts of parental involvement in the literature: a rose-tinted perspective?

Finally, Vincent (1996) is critical of the way that relationships between parents and schools are reported by some writers, arguing that discussion of home–school links in published research tends to be cursory and shallow. She is concerned that written accounts that are characterized by a 'cheery, unfailingly positive tone' (p. 74) contribute to an erroneous perception that home–school relations are uncomplicated and unproblematic. Apart from being misleading, such 'rose-tinted' reports can result in individuals feeling disillusioned and blameworthy if similar results are not achieved. Another concern relates to the prevalent assumption that parents' involvement in schooling inevitably results in improvements in children's achievement. Vincent argues that the **type** of parental involvement that results in such improvements is unclear. She also suggests that the duration of some intervention projects that claim to improve children's achievement may be rather brief. Although parents may well be able to sustain motivated involvement for short periods of time, such involvement and the resulting improvements in their children's learning may be only temporary. Yet another criticism relates to the danger that certain initiatives might present a fashionable 'answer' to the challenge of home–school links. As an example, Vincent discusses the trend in the 1980s for schools to create parents' rooms in schools. She argues that although such rooms can provide a hospitable space for parents to meet, their success ultimately depends on the existence of a welcoming ethos within the school.

Conclusions

In this chapter, attention has been drawn to some of the key problems that permeate the field of family involvement, with commentary on tensions that may result when certain parents are described as being 'hard to reach'. Although such problems may be caused by insensitive terminology, in many respects it goes deeper than this – some difficulties may be exacerbated by the assumptions and beliefs that underpin the terms used by professionals and researchers. Such assumptions may be well intended, but they may also be insensitive to the needs of families and children, and may inadvertently undermine and demean those to whom they are applied. The core theme that emerges in this analysis is that parental engagement is often more nuanced and more complex than it may initially appear.

Another important implication of the discussion in this chapter is that attention needs to shift away from labelling some parents as 'hard to reach', and focus more on how schools can become more reachable. This is the subject of the final chapter.

7

Creating More Approachable Schools and Other Settings

Introduction

This chapter explores how schools and other settings can make themselves more open and 'reachable'. First, there is commentary on parents having confidence when approaching teachers and other professionals and on the importance of developing a sense of self-efficacy and agency. Then there is discussion of the value of schools finding out details of parents' strengths and needs in order that collaborative initiatives are carefully matched to families' profiles. This is followed by commentary on Susan Swap's partnership model and on the value of using materials such as the *Index for Inclusion* to elicit parents' views about schools. Finally, there is discussion of the relevance of social capital and sociocultural theory, with commentary on implications for teachers aiming to engage parents who might be described as hard to reach.

Engaging 'Hard to Reach' Parents: Teacher–Parent Collaboration to Promote Children's Learning By Anthony Feiler © 2010 John Wiley & Sons, Ltd

Parents' sense of self-belief and agency

Conceptualizing some families as being difficult to engage is, to a certain extent, a reflection of viewpoints about difference. Thomas and Loxley (2001) discuss the link between difference and diversity, arguing effectively that assumptions about 'differences from the norm' are very much influenced by the perspectives of those making such judgements. These authors propose that whether differences are interpreted negatively or positively depends on the outlook adopted by those forming such judgements:

RESEARCH QUOTATION

'Difference and identity are constructed in and through social relations. Whether difference is seen positively, as diversity, or negatively as deviance or deficit depends on the mindset of the person or group of people who observe that difference.'

Thomas and Loxley, 2001, p. 93

If parents feel that diversity is viewed as a deficit and do not feel respected and valued, it is likely that this will impact on their sense of self-efficacy and on their confidence in relation to educational professionals. Parental levels of self-belief and agency are likely to influence both the amount and quality of parental engagement with schools – if parents feel hesitant about their own knowledge and skills in relation to the curriculum, pedagogy and education in general, this may undermine their willingness to collaborate with teachers and other educational staff. One of the most compelling discussions of the factors that contribute to adults' feelings of self-worth and agency is presented by Bandura (1997). He suggests that self-efficacy beliefs are constructed from certain key sources which include direct experience (enactive mastery) and learning from others (vicarious experiences):

Enactive mastery. A key factor in the development of agency or self-efficacy is direct, personal experiences of 'mastery'. Bandura asserts that this is the most influential source of efficacy information, as it provides authentic evidence of whether one has what it takes to succeed (knowledge, skills, determination and so forth). The implication is that sufficient amounts of support and scaffolding need to be built into parental engagement schemes to ensure that those involved experience a concrete level of accomplishment. This might entail providing tangible feedback to parents about what has been achieved, particularly during the early phases of a parent engagement initiative.

Vicarious experiences. For many activities, there are no absolute measures of adequacy and people need to appraise their capabilities in relation to others. Bandura suggests that learning from others is a principal source of self-efficacy, and comparison with others plays a central part in our perceived self-efficacy. One implication is that parental engagement initiatives might be structured in such a way that **groups** of parents are involved so that a 'community of practice' (Lave and Wenger, 1991) can be established, with parents learning with and from each other.

The need to respond to diversity

One way for schools to communicate a positive message of respect to parents and to emphasize that they are valued is to ensure that events and processes are vigilantly tailored to their needs. The core theme of this book is that initiatives to promote collaboration between parents and schools are unlikely to be readily available or 'off the shelf' – they need to be carefully thought through and specially devised for particular settings and particular groups. Carpenter and Lall (2005) report on four projects in London secondary schools which aimed to involve parents in their children's learning and which were specifically designed for local circumstances. The authors emphasize that each school had a particular set of so-called hard to reach parents. They conclude that it is vital for school staff to work in close collaboration with parents to establish which specific barriers impact on particular groups of parents and to ensure that these are addressed:

RESEARCH QUOTATION

'The central point here is that a "one size fits all" policy is not an option and that the preparation and the organisation of a project must be conceived as an interface between the school and those particular targeted parents and their specific external environment.'

Carpenter and Lall, 2005, p. 34

Carpenter and Lall found that certain features common to these projects seemed to underpin their success in engaging 'hard to reach' parents – three of these aspects are summarized below:

Active support from senior staff. It is important that staff and senior management embrace parent engagement initiatives enthusiastically and are seen to be actively supportive. This is especially the case when dealing with difficult issues such as racial equality.

Flexibility, self-evaluation and bottom-up initiatives. Flexibility is key to the development of effective initiatives so that teachers can be responsive to the needs of the families. The effects of a parental engagement programme need to be continuously appraised. Locally devised initiatives that address local problems are more successful than projects that originate from outside the school.

Supporting parental access to the activities. If organizational arrangements are dealt with effectively, parents can be supported to access meetings and other events. This may be particularly important with 'hard to reach' parents who may value help with childcare or the provision of translated communications. Small adjustments such as changing a meeting time to suit parents' work-time constraints can have a marked impact on parental engagement.

Another example of the need to design strategies that closely reflect the needs of particular schools and particular communities comes from the Home–School Knowledge Exchange project (Feiler et al., 2006) discussed earlier in this book. In this study, it became apparent that not all activities which aimed to enhance home–school collaboration appealed to all parents – different approaches to engaging and valuing parents were needed for different schools. Each home–school activity evolved from factors arising in particular schools and communities and was designed in response to particular issues raised by teachers and parents. To a large extent, the activities were context specific – specific to particular teachers and groups of parents, and to particular issues in certain schools and communities. The implication is that when schools develop activities for enhancing the exchange of information between teachers and families, it is important that these activities reflect and are responsive to local circumstances.

Home–school partnership models should lay a foundation for establishing inclusive relationships between teachers and parents, frameworks in which there is scope for negotiation and cooperation so that developments are fine-tuned to the needs of schools and families. A range of frameworks for collaborative work between teachers and parents have been proposed, and a detailed discussion of contrasting home–school models is presented in Swap's book (1993) *Developing Home–School Partnerships: From Concepts to Practice*.

Home–school collaboration models

In her book on parent–teacher collaboration, Swap presents four models of home–school relations (Box 7.1).

Box 7.1 Susan Swap's models of home–school relations (Swap, 1993).

1. **The protective model.** This model separates teachers' and parents' roles, and its primary aim is to shield or protect teachers from 'interference' from parents. Three key assumptions underpin this model: parents hand over responsibility for educating their children to the school, teachers concur

(continued)

with the allocation of this responsibility and the corollary is that parents view teachers as answerable for children's learning outcomes.

2. **The school-to-home transmission model.** There is recognition that parents' active involvement in children's learning contributes to higher achievement, and teachers view parents as a valuable resource in transmitting school values and skills to children. The aim of this model is to secure parental help to support the goals of the school, with the direction of contact being from teachers to parents.

3. **The curriculum enrichment model.** Schools aim to develop the curriculum so that it reflects more fully the values, history and culture of the various communities it serves. Where there is continuity between children's home and school cultures, it is more likely that learning will improve; it is acknowledged that many parents have expertise and skills that can broaden and augment the curriculum.

4. **The partnership model.** With this framework, collaborative relationships between parents and teachers impact on **all** aspects of the school's ethos, where 'children are working hard, succeeding academically, and feeling good about themselves; where teachers are working enthusiastically with each other, with administration, and with other resource persons to figure out even better ways to reach all the children; where parents and grandparents are champions of the school and committed to working with educators toward a common mission; where community resources enrich the school's curriculum and provide support to the staff' (Swap, 1993, p. 67). This model is discussed in more detail in the text below.

Swap's partnership model

Although Swap does not claim that the partnership model will be desirable or appropriate for **all** schools, she suggests that it might be the model of choice for schools facing the following challenges: schools where most children are not achieving well, schools where families are relatively heterogeneous and schools where there is a lack of consensus between teachers and parents about what constitutes 'success' for students. Swap emphasizes that in the partnership model the term 'parents' includes not only a child's biological mother and father but also step-parents, grandparents and any other relative or person who plays a role in providing primary care and has a special relationship with the child. Swap's partnership model is characterized by an extensive collaboration between teachers and parents that pervades the entirety of the school's culture. It comprises four elements, each of which resonates with frameworks and projects discussed in the previous chapters.

Creating two-way communication between homes and schools. Swap views two-way communication as fundamental to the development of sound school–home partnerships. Both parents and teachers have particular information they can share about children, and the aim of this strand of the model is to produce a rich, two-way exchange between parents and educators. It is suggested that this interchange is often best achieved by creating informal gatherings and social events during which 'socialising, fun, [and] good food' (Swap, 1993, p. 67) signal a caring attitude, and which provide opportunities for joint communication between parents and staff. The *Drop in for Coffee* scheme in Scotland (discussed in Chapter 4) is an example of such an initiative; the informality of this approach helped to put parents more at ease and dissolve uncertainties and suspicions. Swap suggests that three core features indicate that effective two-way communication is developing: (1) more families are involved than in the past, (2) families are involved in a wide range of activities for long enough to make a difference and (3) both education staff and parents see involvement as productive and purposeful.

Enhancing children's learning at school and at home. Swap argues that the primary aim of developing a partnership between schools and homes is to improve children's learning. This might entail creating opportunities for parents to help at school – for example as volunteers or learning mentors. The INSPIRE scheme (Chapter 4) is an outstanding example of parents contributing directly to children's learning at school through invitations from their child to participate in school-based workshops on reading or mathematics. Furthermore, Swap argues that improving children's learning might well necessitate enhanced support at home – for example, teachers might review homework demands to ensure that they are clear to the child and to parents.

Providing mutual support. Swap suggests that parents and teachers being mutually supportive of each other can have a powerful impact on children's learning. She points out that there are numerous opportunities for schools and parents to provide such reciprocal support. These might include focusing on developments and activities that enhance children's learning, or schools may focus more directly on supporting parents' own educational needs and interests, thus helping children's development indirectly. For example, schools are well positioned to organize training sessions for parents in computer skills, learning English as an additional language, keeping fit and so forth. Conversely, parents can provide support for school staff. Swap gives an example of parents overtly celebrating teachers' work: 'Thank you letters, occasional articles in the local newspaper that explain a teachers' special programme or approach (especially with pictures), a regular education column in the local newspaper that highlights educators' efforts, and an appreciative note to the superintendent about a teacher, with a copy to the teacher, are all examples of ways to convey support to educators as professionals and individuals' (Swap, 1993, p. 131).

Making joint decisions. A critical feature of a productive relationship between schools and families is the creation of opportunities for parents not only to contribute to their own child's learning but also to become involved in management and decision-making at the school. It is notoriously difficult to encourage parents to participate in school committees and meetings; however, Swap points out that where this occurs, particularly where parents are involved in decision-making that impacts on the core features of schooling such as the curriculum and choice of teaching methods, the outcome can be immensely productive. In Chapter 3 we discussed the CoZi model of parental involvement and how parents contributed to school governance – decision-making was participatory and parents were viewed as playing an integral role in this process.

Allen (2007) suggests that an important factor in developing the sort of authentic home–school partnership described by Swap (1993) is teachers' willingness to transform schools by establishing collaborations that are 'culturally grounded', that is, school–home links that take account of and build on the diversity of family and community practices. This means teachers finding out about family and community practices within a particular neighbourhood. Allen emphasizes that knowledge of such practices cannot be guessed at or based on stereotypical viewpoints that fix on a few, assumed core characteristics of certain groups. Rather, culturally responsive relationships are founded on knowledge that has to be gained by staff actively reaching out and discovering from direct contact with parents what motivates them, what aspirations they hold for their children and what knowledge and skills families have acquired. It is suggested that information might be gained from parents through question-naires that could be discussed and designed with children (Box 7.2).

Box 7.2   Family survey: seeking information from parents about home practices and skills (adapted from Allen, 2007).

Literacy and linguistic knowledge. What languages or dialects are spoken at home? What kinds of written and visual languages are in use, for example favourite books, poems or songs, news-papers, DVDs/videos? Does the whole family watch any television programmes together?

Pedagogical knowledge. How do children learn out of school? What kinds of games do they play? Do children have respon-sibility for caring for pets or other animals? What supports or barriers affect children's out of school learning? Which people help children to learn at home?

Parents' knowledge. What work-related skills do parents have; for example childcare, management, culinary, cleaning skills, etc.? What other skills do parents have; for example musical, horticul-tural, etc.?

Community knowledge. What informal or formal community groups are important for families, for example sport, church, etc.?

Knowledge beyond the local community. Do families travel to visit relatives in other parts of the country, or in other countries? What do parents feel children learn from such visits?

The importance of actively seeking parents' views is similarly emphasized in materials that have been developed in the United Kingdom, the *Index for Inclusion*.

The Index for Inclusion

The *Index for Inclusion* (*Index* for short) was developed in the United Kingdom by Tony Booth and Mel Ainscow, in collaboration with Mark Vaughan (Booth and Ainscow, 2002). It is a practical tool devised for teachers to map inclusive practice in schools, to decide on priorities, to implement change and to review the impact of these changes. One of its principal sections is devoted to partnership between staff and parents/carers. The *Index* is of relevance internationally where there is enthusiasm for developing more inclusive schools, and these materials have been adapted for use in approximately 25 countries (Booth and Black-Hawkins, 2005).

The *Index* framework and materials enable staff in schools to conduct a process of self-review and improvement by exploring the views of staff, students and parents/carers. The term 'barriers to learning and participation' provides an alternative to the more deficit-oriented concept of special educational needs, and the aim of these materials is to enable school staff to explore how such barriers can be reduced for **all** students. A 'review–implement–evaluate' cycle is presented, which includes gathering and reviewing information about the school, devising an inclusive school development plan, implementing priorities and evaluating progress.

Much of the *Index* is devoted to the initial review step in this cycle (gathering information about the school), and materials are presented for exploring current practice and perspectives related to three dimensions: the development of inclusive cultures, policies, and practices. One of the sections comprising the development of inclusive cultures is 'Building community'. This section is particularly relevant as it includes a focus on schools developing collaborative relations with parents/carers. This aspect encompasses an overarching statement of aspiration about building a partnership between staff and parents/carers, together with questions to help schools compare existing provision with this goal. Box 7.3 lists questions that school staff may wish to consider when reviewing their relations with parents.

Box 7.3   Items from the *Index for Inclusion*, 'Building community: there is partnership between staff and parents/carers' (Booth and Ainscow, 2002, p. 46).

- Do parents/carers and staff respect each other?
- Do parents/carers feel that there is good communication with staff?
- Are all parents/carers well informed about school policies and practices?
- Are parents/carers aware of the priorities in the school development plan?
- Are all parents/carers given an opportunity to be involved in decisions made about the school?
- Are the fears that some parents/carers have about coming into school and meeting teachers recognized and steps taken to overcome them?
- Is there a variety of opportunities for parents/carers to become involved in the school?
- Is there a variety of occasions when parents/carers can discuss the progress of, and concerns about, their children?
- Are the different contributions that parents/carers can make to the school equally appreciated?
- Do staff value the knowledge that parents/carers have about their children?
- Do staff encourage the involvement of all parents/carers in their children's learning?
- Are parents/carers clear about what they can do to support their children's learning at home?
- Do all parents/carers feel that their children are valued by the school?
- Do all parents/carers feel that their concerns are taken seriously by the school?

The *Index* includes examples of five questionnaires that schools may use or adapt. One questionnaire is specifically aimed at parents/carers of secondary students, and respondents are asked to indicate whether they definitely agree, agree to some extent or disagree with statements such as the following:

- The information I was given when my child(ren) first came to the school was excellent.
- I think the school keeps me well informed about how my child(ren) is/are doing.
- All families are equally valued whatever their backgrounds.
- Bullying is a problem at the school.
- Staff at this school encourage all students to do their best, not just the most able.

The authors emphasize that it may well be appropriate for school staff and parent representatives to adapt and customize the materials in the *Index* to devise their own purpose-made surveys for parents/carers. Clearly, in many schools it may be necessary for questionnaires to be translated for parents not having English as their first language. Another suggested strategy is for schools to arrange group meetings with parents to explore families' perspectives, and the authors suggest that such groups might start by considering three general questions:

- What would help to improve the learning of your child in this school?
- What could be done to make your child happier in school?
- What would you most like to change about this school?

In order to increase the level of participation and to engage so-called harder to reach parents, such meetings could take place in settings away from school, and a variety of different times and days of the week could be offered. A parent/carer questionnaire could be sent to parents/carers after the meeting so as to elicit the views of those who were unable to attend.

The *Index for Inclusion* presents a practical set of materials that can be used by a wide range of schools in different contexts. The pack includes suggestions for tackling complex processes such as how to initiate a review of practice, and there is a welcome flexibility that enables schools to adjust approaches in order to suit local circumstances.

Engaging hard to reach parents and the contribution of social capital and sociocultural theory

Researchers' and policy makers' interest in the concept of social capital was introduced in Chapter 1, and it has been referred to at various points in the book. Social capital is broadly defined as the network of formal and informal contacts developed amongst those with shared outlooks. The UK's Office for National Statistics suggests that social capital matters because higher levels of social capital tend to be associated with improved health, better employment outcomes, lower crime rates and increased educational achievement (www.statistics.gov.uk). Social capital has been of particular interest to those exploring variations in families' engagement with education and is, therefore, highly relevant to the focus of this book. Bourdieu (1986) suggests that families differ considerably in terms of the form of social capital that he terms **cultural** capital. This includes the values and perspectives that individuals develop early on during their upbringing, which may later be reflected in our educational qualifications, in the way we talk to or address others and in our aims and expectations. Differing levels of cultural capital tend to impact on parents' confidence when approaching teachers or other members of the school staff. Parents with poor educational experiences and low formal achievement levels are likely to be at a disadvantage when questioning educational decisions, or when discussing the curriculum or pedagogy with school staff. They may lack confidence in their ability to contribute to their child's learning and may experience a range of difficulties in engaging with education. This may cause some parents to withdraw from certain aspects of collaboration with schools, which in turn may result in teachers viewing some parents as hard to reach. A number of key questions arise when initiatives aimed at engaging hard to reach parents are examined from a social and cultural capital perspective:

- How far do schools recognize families' social and cultural capital? Some families may have a wide range of skills and knowledge that may not be directly reflected in the curriculum. These abilities may include experiences of the building trade, skills in retailing and accounting or depth of knowledge about different cultural traditions and customs. Such 'funds of knowledge' (Moll et al., 1992) could contribute to Swap's vision of the curriculum enrichment model, where aspects of the syllabus are amended so that they resonate with families' expertise and know-how.

- Do teachers have different kinds of social and cultural capital to that of the parents in the local community? Where there are marked differences between teachers' and parents' levels of education, social background and income, it may be more difficult for teachers to relate to the lifestyles of some parents, just as it may be harder for some parents to share the values and social outlook of the teachers. This division may be more likely to develop when schools are located in areas where there are high levels of deprivation and poverty and when teachers do not live in the immediate catchment area served by their school. In such circumstances, there may be a role for other school staff – such as teaching assistants – to form bridges between schools and communities, as such staff may live locally and may have formed close contacts with families over generations.

- How can schools contribute to the social capital that families may depend upon? Schools have considerable potential to enhance the range and quality of social connections that families develop. They are a 'constant' in the lives of most families, providing stability and continuity for children and parents over many years. Because of their role in the community, schools can provide valuable opportunities for parents to connect with other parents who share similar or differing interests, and to develop cultural, occupational or leisure-related skills that may be of direct and substantial benefit, particularly to families who may be hard for schools to reach. Some teachers may resist the development of extended schools that offer keep-fit classes for parents, computer skills workshops or English speaking/writing sessions. They may oppose such initiatives, viewing them as being beyond the scope of teachers' professional practice and belonging more to the realm of social work. However, the value that such opportunities provide may be substantial: they may boost families' social capital, enhancing families' connections within the community and with the school, and such opportunities may have a direct impact on children's learning and social development.

This book has endeavoured to answer the question why schools need to engage with parents, particularly those who are perceived as being hard to reach. Social capital theory proposes that the relationships we build up provide patterns of mutual support that make our lives more rewarding and productive. These connections result in benefits that promote our personal and communal interests. A key challenge is for schools to recognize the importance of reaching out to all parents, however diverse their backgrounds and cultural differences, so that these links can contribute to the development of families' networks and social relationships.

The second theoretical strand that has underpinned many examples of home–school collaboration in this book is sociocultural theory. This perspective illuminates the vital role played by adults and more knowledgeable others, both at school and at home, in scaffolding children's thinking and learning. The projects presented in this book reflect principal aspects of this perspective on children's development, acknowledging that young people are more likely to learn and develop when there is effective, flexible collaboration between parents and teachers. Barbara Rogoff's research and writing have extended our understanding of sociocultural theory. She suggests that through a process of 'guided participation' parents help children acquire values, skills and practices and learn to take on new roles and responsibilities (Rogoff, 2003). She argues that whether or not what children learn through guided participation is seen by society as desirable, the role played by parents in this general process is similar across societies around the world. For example, Rogoff explains how Guatemalan Mayan indigenous girls learn to make corn meal pancakes through a carefully staged participative process. Initially the young girls watch their mothers. Then they are given a small lump of dough and their mothers help them to compress and flatten it. Later, verbal prompts and demonstrations are provided by the mothers to assist their daughters. In an example from the West, Rogoff refers to the strategies used by middle-class parents when looking at a picture book with young children. The form of assistance provided – for example the prompts used and the way questions are posed – is adjusted carefully to match the child's developmental stage and level of understanding in the same way that Guatemalan Mayan mothers help their daughters learn how to make tortillas (Rogoff, 2003). The accounts provided by scholars like Rogoff provide compelling examples of the abundance of skill, patience and diligence used by parents when supporting their children's learning. To overlook this form of expertise and assistance when pedagogic planning is under way is a wasted opportunity.

Conclusions

In 2006/2007 inspectors from the Office for Standards in Education conducted research into UK primary and secondary practices to evaluate how schools set about involving parents and carers. In their report *Parents, Carers and Schools*, it emerged that the most effective schools showed 'versatility, flexibility and determination' in their efforts to engage with families: 'These schools identified precisely how the parents could contribute, evaluated the impact of initiatives and, if they had not worked, changed the way in which they promoted them until they did work' (Office for Standards in Education, 2007, p. 4). In the UK government's recent draft policy document *Analysis and Evidence Strategy* (Department for Children, Schools and Families, 2008), there is a welcome statement about the need to conduct similar research to improve our understanding of how to engage parents who may be 'hard to reach' through children's centres, extended schools and other services. It is apparent that the importance of schools developing constructive, two-way relationships with families has been recognized. This message can also be found on government web sites about parents such as the Qualifications and Curriculum Authority's (2008) 'Partnership with Parents' (www.qca.org.uk), where it is emphasized that in order to secure effective links between parents and schools, a welcoming culture is needed. It is suggested that such an ethos can be built up by making all parents feel that they have a positive role to play in their child's education and by demonstrating that parents' linguistic, cultural and religious backgrounds are valued.

Despite such official recognition of the key role parents play in supporting children's learning, it is important to remember the extent to which some parents feel diffident about approaching schools. In her inspiring book *Creating Welcoming Schools*, Allen (2007) presents insightful guidelines for conversations between teachers and parents, which come 'straight from my parent and grandparent heart' and are addressed to a child's teacher:

- I'd love to chat with you. I'd enjoy knowing you better and learning more about you, and then I'd be willing to tell you more about myself.

- Please don't ask me 'judgement' questions – you know, like how much I read to my child, or if I take her to the library 'regularly', or what time he goes to bed. I know what you want to hear. I'll either lie or avoid the question. If you'll excuse my bluntness, it really isn't any of your business. Of course, some of that might come out in a conversation – you have trouble getting your kid away from the TV, too? Let's talk.

- I love talking about my child, as long as I feel we are both considering his best interests. I will shut down if you tell me she is lazy, disabled, too loud, too quiet – just about any label. I'll listen carefully if you tell me stories about my child in your classroom; maybe we can talk together about how we both interpret those stories.

- I'll solve problems with you – these are my children, and nothing is more important to me, whether I show that to you or not. We can brainstorm options, discuss pros and cons, and come up with plans where we all have a part – you, me, and my child. If you come in with a 'solution' and just want me to sign something, I probably won't.

What is notable from the examples discussed in previous chapters is that even in the most unpromising circumstances, parents are able to provide impressive levels of support. Even when parents face barriers in engaging with schools, or when they live in poverty or have experienced a poor quality of education themselves, there are still inspirational examples of parents supporting their children's learning, often with the active support of teachers who have reached out to such families and who have been successful in making schools more approachable.

References

Allen, J. (2007) *Creating Welcoming Schools: A Practical Guide to Home–School Partnerships with Diverse Families*, Teachers College Press, New York.

Audit Commission (2002) *Special Educational Needs: A Mainstream Issue*, Audit Commission, London.

Avramidis, E. and Norwich, B. (2003) Promoting inclusive education: a review of literature on teachers' attitudes towards integration and inclusion, in *Learning to Read Critically in Teaching and Learning* (eds L. Poulson and M. Wallace), Sage, London, pp. 201–222.

Ball, S.J. (2003) *Class Strategies and the Educational Market: The Middle-Classes and Social Advantage*, RoutledgeFalmer, London.

Bandura, A. (1997) *Self-Efficacy: The Exercise of Control*, Freeman, New York.

Barton, A., Drake, C., Perez, J., St-Louis, K. and George, M. (2004) Ecologies of parental engagement in urban education. *Educational Researcher*, **33** (4), 3–12.

Bastiani, J. and White, S. (2003) *Involving Parents, Raising Achievement*. Department for Education and Skills, London.

Bateson, B. (2000) INSPIRE, in *The Contribution of Parents to School Effectiveness* (eds S. Wolfendale and J. Bastiani), David Fulton, London, pp. 52–68.

Besag, F.M.C. (2002) Childhood epilepsy in relation to mental handicap and behavioural disorders. *Journal of Child Psychology and Psychiatry*, **43** (1), 103–131.

Engaging 'Hard to Reach' Parents: Teacher–Parent Collaboration to Promote Children's Learning By Anthony Feiler © 2010 John Wiley & Sons, Ltd

Beveridge, S. (2005) *Children, Families and Schools: Developing Partnerships for Inclusive Education*, RoutledgeFalmer, London.

Bhopal, K. (2004) Gypsy travellers and education: changing needs and changing perceptions. *British Journal of Educational Studies*, **52** (1), 47–64.

Bhopal, K. and Myers, M. (2008) *Insiders, Outsiders and Others: Gypsies and Identity*, University of Hertfordshire Press, Hertfordshire.

Blank, M.J. (2003) Educational reform: the community school approach, in *Promising Practices to Connect Schools with the Community* (ed. D.B. Hiatt-Michael), Information Age, Greenwich, CT, pp. 9–33.

Boethel, M. (2003) *Diversity: School, Family and Community Connections*, National Center for Family and Community Connections with Schools, Austin, TX.

Booth, T. and Ainscow, M. (2002) *The Index for Inclusion: Developing Learning and Participation in Schools*, The Centre for Studies on Inclusive Education, Bristol.

Booth, T. and Black-Hawkins, K. (2005) *Developing Learning and Participation in Countries of the South: The Role of an Index for Inclusion*, UNESCO, Paris, www.csie.org.uk (accessed 27 February 2009).

Bourdieu, P. (1986) The forms of capital, in *Handbook of Theory and Research for the Sociology of Education* (ed. J. Richardson), Greenwood Press, New York, pp. 241–258.

Broadhurst, K., Paton, H. and May-Chahal, C. (2005) Children missing from school systems: exploring divergent patterns of disengagement in the narrative accounts of parents, carers, children and young people. *British Journal of Sociology of Education*, **26** (1), 105–119.

Buchanan, A., Bennett, F., Ritchie, C., Smith, T., Smith, G., Harker, L. and Vitali-Ebers, S. (2004) *The Impact of Government Policy on Social Exclusion among Children aged 0–13 and Their Families*, Social Exclusion Unit, London.

Cabinet Office (2006) *Reaching Out: An Action Plan on Social Exclusion*, Cabinet Office, London.

Caddell, D., Crowther, J., O'Hara, P. and Tett, L. (2000) Investigating the roles of parents and schools in children's early years education. Paper presented at the *European Conference on Educational Research*, Edinburgh.

Cairney, T. (2003) Literacy within family life, in *Handbook of Early Childhood Literacy* (eds N. Hall, J. Larson and J. Marsh), Sage, London, pp. 85–98.

Carpenter, V. and Lall, M. (2005) *Review of Successful Parental Involvement Practice for 'Hard to Reach' Parents*, The London Institute of Education, London.

Carr, M. (2001) *Assessment in Early Childhood Settings: Learning Stories*, Paul Chapman, London.

Carvalho, M. (2001) *Rethinking Family-School Relations: A Critique of Parental Involvement*, Lawrence Erlbaum Associates, Mahwah, NJ.

Charman, T. and Baird, G. (2002) Practitioner review: diagnosis of autism spectrum disorder in 2- and 3-year old children. *Journal of Child Psychology and Psychiatry*, **43** (3), 289–305.

Coffield, F., Robinson, P. and Sarsby, J. (1980) *A Cycle of Deprivation? A Case Study of Four Families*, Heinemann Educational Books, London.

Comer, J. (1980) *School Power*, Free Press, New York.

Crozier, G. (2000) *Parents and Schools: Partners or Protagonists?* Trentham Books, Stoke on Trent.

Crozier, G. (2001) Excluded parents: the deracialisation of parental involvement. *Race, Ethnicity and Education*, **4** (4), 329–341.

Crozier, G. (2004) *End of Award Report, Parents, Children and the School Experience: Asian Families' Perspectives*, www.sunderland.ac.uk (accessed 4 September 2008).

Crozier, G. and Reay, D. (eds.) (2005) *Activating Participation: Parents and Teachers Working Together towards Partnership*, Trentham Books, Stoke on Trent.

Cummins, J. (1986) Empowering minority students: a framework for intervention. *Harvard Educational Review*, **56** (1), 18–36.

Cummins, J. (2001) Empowering minority students: a framework for intervention. Author's introduction: framing the universe of discourse: Are the constructs of power and identity relevant to school failure? *Harvard Educational Review*, **71** (4), 649–655.

Cunningham, C. and Davis, H. (1985) *Working with Parents: Frameworks for Collaboration*, Open University Press, Milton Keynes.

D'Addio, C. (2007) *Intergenerational Transmission of Disadvantage: Mobility or Immobility across Generations? A Review of the Evidence for OECD Countries*, OECD, Paris.

Department for Children, Schools and Families (2008) *Draft Analysis and Evidence Policy*, Department for Children, Schools and Families, London.

Department for Education and Science (DES) (1967) *The Plowden Report: Children and their Primary Schools – A Report of the Central Advisory Council for Education (England)*, Her Majesty's Stationery Office, London.

Department for Education and Skills (2001) *The Special Educational Needs Code of Practice*, DES Publications, Nottingham.

Department for Education and Skills (2003a) *A Better Education for Children in Care*. Social Exclusion Unit Report, Office of the Deputy Prime Minister, London.

Department for Education and Skills (2003b) *Aiming High: Raising the Achievement of Gypsy Traveller Pupils. A Guide to Good Practice*, DES Publications, London.

Department for Education and Skills (2003c) *Every Child Matters*, DES Publications, London.

Department for Education and Skills (2003d) *Every Child Matters: Change for Children in Schools*, DES Publications, Nottingham.

Department for Education and Skills (2004a) *Aiming High: Guidance on Supporting the Education of Asylum Seeking and Refugee Children*, DES Publications, Nottingham.

Department for Education and Skills (2004b) *Engaging Fathers: Involving Parents, Raising Achievement*, DES Publications, Nottingham.

Department for Education and Skills (2004c) *Every Child Matters: Change for Children*, Stationery Office, London.

Department for Education and Skills (2004d) *Every Child Matters: Change for Children in Schools*, DES Publications, Nottingham.

Department for Education and Skills (2004e) *Removing Barriers to Achievement*, DES Publications, Nottingham.

Department for Education and Skills (2005a) *Aiming High: Partnerships between Schools and Traveller Education Support Services in Raising the Achievement of Gypsy Traveller Pupils*, DES Publications, Nottingham.

Department for Education and Skills (2005b) *Support for Parents: Best Start for Children*, The Stationery Office, London.

Department for Education and Skills (2006) *Care Matters: Transforming the Lives of Children and Young People in Care*, DES Publications, Nottingham.

Department for Education and Skills (2007a) *Care Matters: Time for Change (White Paper)*, The Stationery Office, London.

Department for Education and Skills (2007b) *Extended Schools: Building on Experience*, DES Publications, Nottingham.

Department for Children, Schools and Families (2008) *Care Matters: Time to Deliver for Children in Care*, Department for Children, Schools and Families Publications, Nottingham.

Derrington, C. and Kendall, S. (2004) *Gypsy Traveller Students in Secondary Schools: Culture, Identity and Achievement*, Trentham Books, Stoke on Trent.

Desforges, C. and Abouchaar, A. (2003) *The Impact of Parental Involvement, Parental Support and Family Education on Pupil Achievement and Adjustment: A Literature Review*, Department for Education and Skills, Nottingham.

Desimone, L., Finn-Stevenson, M. and Henrich, C. (2000). Whole school reform in a low-income African American community: the effects of the CoZi Model on teachers, parents, and students. *Urban Education*, **35** (3), 269–323.

Doherty, P., Stott, A. and Kinder, K. (2004) *Delivering Services to Hard to Reach Families in On Track Areas: Definition, Consultation and Needs Assessment*, Home Office, London.

Dyson, A. and Robson, E. (1999) *School, Family, Community: Mapping School Inclusion in the UK*, Youth Work Press, Leicester.

Dyson, L. (1993) Response to the presence of a child with disabilities. *American Journal of Mental Retardation*, **98** (2), 207–218.

Edwards, A. and Warin, J. (1999) Parental involvement in raising the achievement of primary school pupils: why bother? *Oxford Review of Education*, **25** (3), 325–341.

Edwards, C.P. (2003) 'Fine designs' from Italy: Montessori education and the Reggio approach. *Montessori Life*, **15** (1), 33–38.

Epstein, J. (2001) *School, Family and Community Partnerships: Preparing Educators and Improving Schools*, Westview Press, Oxford.

Erwin, E. and Soodak, L. (2008) The evolving relationship between families of children with disabilities and professionals, in *Education for All: Critical Issues in the Education of Children and Youth with Disabilities* (eds T. Jiménez and V. Graf), Jossey-Bass, San Francisco, CA, pp. 35–70.

Feiler, A. (2005) Linking home and school literacy in an inner city reception class. *Journal of Early Childhood Literacy*, **5** (2), 131–149.

Feiler, A., Andrews, J., Greenhough, P., Hughes, M., Johnson, D., Scanlan, M. and Ching Yee, W. (2007) *Improving Primary Literacy: Linking Home and School*, RoutledgeFalmer, Abingdon.

Feiler, A., Andrews, J., Greenhough, P., Hughes, M., Johnson, D., Scanlan, M. and Yee, W. (2008) The home school knowledge exchange project: linking home and school to improve children's literacy. *Support for Learning*, **23** (1), 12–18.

Feiler, A., Greenhough, P., Winter, J., Salway, L. and Scanlan, M. (2006) Getting engaged: possibilities and problems for home school knowledge exchange. *Educational Review*, **58** (4), 451–469.

Feiler, A. and Logan, E. (2007) The literacy early action project (LEAP): exploring factors underpinning a child's progress with literacy during his first year at school. *The British Journal of Special Education*, **34** (3), 162–169.

Frederickson, N. and Cline, T. (2002) *Special Educational Needs, Inclusion and Diversity: A Textbook*, Open University Press, Buckingham.

Gillborn, D. and Mirza, H. (2000) *Educational Inequality: Mapping Race, Class and Gender – A Synthesis of Research Evidence*, Office for Standards in Education, London.

Glass, N. (1999) Sure Start: The development of an early intervention programme for young children in the United Kingdom. *Children and Society*, **13** (4), 257–264.

Gregory, E. and Williams, A. (2004) Living literacies in homes and communities, in *The RoutledgeFalmer Reader in Language and Literacy* (ed. T. Grainger), RoutledgeFalmer, London, pp. 33–51.

Harker, R. (2004) More than the sum of its parts? Inter-professional working in the education of looked after children. *Children and Society*, **18** (3), 179–193.

Harris, A. and Goodall, J. (2007) *Engaging Parents in Raising Achievement: Do Parents Know They Matter?* University of Warwick, Warwick.

Hart, J.T. (1971) The inverse care law. *Lancet*, **i**, 405–12.

Hately-Broad, B. (2004) Problems and good practice in post-compulsory educational provision for travellers: the Wakefield Kushti project. *Intercultural Education*, **15** (3), 267–281.

Her Majesty's Stationery Office (1978) *The Report of the Committee of Enquiry into the Education of Handicapped Children and Young People (the Warnock Report)*, Her Majesty's Stationery Office, London.

Hiatt-Michael, D. (2003) The emerging community school concept in the USA, in *School, Family, and Community Partnership in a World of Differences and Changes* (eds S. Castelli, M. Mendel and B. Ravn), Wydawnictwo Uniwersytetu Gdanskiego, Gdansk, pp. 24–50.

Hill, N. and Taylor, L. (2004) Parental school involvement and children's academic achievement. *Current Directions in Psychological Science*, **13** (4), 161–164.

HM Treasury (2005) *Child Poverty: Fair Funding for Schools – A Review of the Ways in which Local Authorities Fund Schools to Meet the Costs Arising from Social Deprivation amongst Their Pupils*, Department for Children, Schools and Families, London.

Hoover-Dempsey, K. and Sandler, H. (1997) Why do parents become involved in their children's education? *Review of Educational Research*, **67** (1), 3–42.

House of Commons Education and Skills Committee (2006) *Special Educational Needs*, The Stationery Office Limited, London.

Hughes, M. and Greenhough, P. (2003) How can homework help learning? *Topic*, **29** (9), 1–5.

Hughes, M. and Pollard, A. (2006) Home–school knowledge exchange in context. *Educational Review*, **58** (4), 385–396.

Humphris, K. (2004) *It's More Than Just a Cup of Coffee: A Collaborative Enquiry – Project Report* (unpublished). University of Dundee, Dundee, http://services.bgfl.org/services (accessed 9 September 2008).

Illsley, P. and Redford, M. (2005) 'Drop in for coffee': working with parents in North Perth New Community Schools. *Support for Learning*, **20** (4), 162–166.

Jacklin, A., Robinson, C. and Torrance, H. (2006) When lack of data is data: do we really know who our looked-after children are? *European Journal of Special Needs Education*, **21** (1), 1–20.

Jackson, K. and Remillard, J. (2005) Rethinking parent involvement: African American mothers construct their roles in Mathematics Education of their children. *School Community Journal*, **15** (1), 51–73.

Jordan, E. (2001) Exclusion of travellers in state schools. *Educational Research*, **43** (2), 117–132.

Karayiannis, C. (2006) Integrating and partnering services in schools – an emerging model in Northern Ireland. *Support for Learning*, **21** (2), 64–69.

Lantoff, J. (2000) Introducing sociocultural theory, in *Sociocultural Theory and Second Language Learning* (ed. J. Lantoff), Oxford University Press, Oxford, pp. 1–26.

Lareau, A. (2000) *Home Advantage: Social Class and Parental Intervention in Elementary School*, Rowman and Littlefield, Oxford.

Lave, J. and Wenger, E. (1991) *Situated Learning: Legitimate Peripheral Participation*, Cambridge University Press, Cambridge.

Leask, J. (2001) Sam's invisible extra gear – a parent's view, in *Experiencing Reggio Emilia: Implications for Pre-School Provision* (eds L. Abbott and C. Nutbrown), Open University Press, Maidenhead, pp. 43–47.

LeBlanc, M. (2008) *Reggio Emilia: An Innovative Approach to Early Childhood Education*, www.communityplaythings.co.uk (accessed 30 May 2008).

Lloyd, G. and Stead J. (2001) 'The boys and girls not calling me names and the teachers to believe me': name calling and the experiences of travellers in school. *Children and Society*, **15** (5), 361–374.

Lochrie, M. (2004) *Family Learning: Building All Our Futures*, National Institute of Adult Continuing Education, Leicester.

Mallett, R. (1997) A parental perspective on partnership, in *Working with Parents of SEN Children after the Code of Practice* (ed. S. Wolfendale), David Fulton, London, pp. 27–40.

Marsh, J. and Millard, E. (2000) *Literacy and Popular Culture: Using Children's Culture in the Classroom*, Paul Chapman, London.

Mattingly, D., Prislin, R., McKenzie, T., Rodriguez, J. and Kayzar, B. (2002) Evaluating evaluations: the case of parental involvement programs. *Review of Educational Research*, **72** (4), 549–576.

McBrien, J. (2005) Educational needs and barriers for refugee students in the United States: a review of the literature. *Review of Educational Research*, **75** (3), 329–364.

McCollum, J. (2002) Influencing the development of young children with disabilities: current themes in early intervention. *Child and Adolescent Mental Health*, **7** (1), 4–9.

McGrath, N. (2007) Engaging the hardest to reach parents in parenting-skills programmes, in *How to Reach 'Hard to Reach' Children: Improving Access, Participation and Outcomes* (eds K. Pomerantz, M. Hughes and D. Thompson), John Wiley & Sons, Ltd, Chichester, pp. 184–205.

McNaughton, S. (2001) Co-constructing expertise: the development of parents' and teachers' ideas about literacy practices and the transition to school. *Journal of Early Childhood Literacy*, **1** (1), 40–58.

Midwinter, E. (1977) The professional-lay relationship: a Victorian legacy. *Journal of Child Psychology and Psychiatry*, **18** (2), 101–113.

Milbourne, L. (2002) Unspoken exclusion: experience of continued marginalisation from education among 'hard to reach' groups of adults and children in the UK. *British Journal of Sociology of Education*, **23** (2), 287–305.

Mittler, P. (2000) *Working towards Inclusive Education: Social Contexts*, David Fulton, London.

Moll, L., Amanti, C., Neff, D. and Gonzalez, N. (1992) Funds of knowledge for teaching: using a qualitative approach to connect homes and classrooms. *Theory Into Practice*, **31** (2), 132–141.

Mongon, D. and Chapman, C. (2008) *Successful Leadership for Promoting the Achievement of White Working Class Pupils*, Nottingham: National College for School Leadership.

Moon, N. and Ivins, C. (2004) *Parental Involvement in Children's Education*, Department for Education and Skills, London.

Muijs, D., Harris, A., Chapman, C. Stoll, L. and Russ, J. (2004) Improving schools in socioeconomically disadvantaged areas: a review of research evidence. *School Effectiveness and School Improvement*, **15** (2), 149–175.

National Assembly for Wales (2000) *Children and Young People: A Framework for Partnership*, National Assembly for Wales, Cardiff.

National Assembly for Wales (2001) *The Learning Country*, National Assembly for Wales, Cardiff.

National Literacy Trust (2001) *Parental Involvement and Literacy Achievement: The Research Evidence and the Way Forward*, National Literacy Trust, London.

National Literacy Trust (2005) *'Every Which Way We Can': A Literacy and Social Inclusion Position Paper*, National Literacy Trust, London.

New, R. (2007) Reggio Emilia as cultural activity theory in practice. *Theory Into Practice* **46** (1), 5–13.

Nutbrown, C., Hannon, P. and Morgan, A. (2005) *Early Literacy Work with Families: Policy, Practice and Research*, Sage, London.

O'Connor, B. (2003) *A Political History of the American Welfare System: When Ideas Have Consequences*, Rowman and Littlefield, Lanham, MD.

Office for Standards in Education (2003) *The Education of Asylum-Seeker Pupils*, Office for Standards in Education, London.

Office for Standards in Education (2004) *Reading for Purpose and Pleasure*, Office for Standards in Education, London.

Office for Standards in Education (2005) *The National Literacy and Numeracy Strategies and the Primary Curriculum*, Office for Standards in Education, London.

Office for Standards in Education (2007) *Parents, Carers and Schools*, Office for Standards in Education, London.

Palmer, G., Macinnes, T. and Kenway, P. (2006) *Monitoring Poverty and Social Exclusion*, Joseph Rowntree Foundation, York.

Performance Indicators in Primary Schools (PIPS Project) (2002) *On-Entry Baseline Assessment 2003 and On-Entry Baseline Assessment: Follow-up*, CEM Centre, University of Durham.

Peters, M., Seeds, K., Goldstein, A. and Coleman, N. (2008) *Parental Involvement in Children's Education*, Department for Children, Schools and Families, London.

Phillips, S. (2001) Special needs or special rights? in *Experiencing Reggio Emilia: Implications for Preschool Provision* (eds L. Abbott and C. Nutbrown), Open University Press, Buckingham, pp. 48–61.

Pomerantz, K., Hughes, M. and Thompson, D. (2007) *How to Reach Hard to Reach Children: Improving Access, Participation and Outcomes*, Wiley-Blackwell, Chichester.

Potter, C. and Whittaker, C. (2001) *Enabling Communication in Children with Autism*, Jessica Kingsley, London.

Power, S. and Clark, A. (2000) The right to know: parents, school reports and parents' evenings. *Research Papers in Education*, **15** (1), 25–48.

Putnam, R. (2000) *Bowling Alone: The Collapse and Revival of American Community*, Simon and Schuster, New York.

Qualifications and Curriculum Development Authority (2008) *Qualifications and Curriculum Authority – Partnership with Parents*, www.qca.org.uk (accessed 8 July 2008).

Reakes, A. and Powell, R. (2004) *The Education of Asylum Seekers in Wales*, The National Foundation for Educational Research, Slough, Berkshire.

Reay, D. (2005) Mothers' involvement in their children's schooling: social reproduction in action? In *Activating Participation: Parents and Teachers Working Together towards Partnership* (eds G. Crozier and D. Reay), Trentham Books, Stoke on Trent, pp. 23–37.

Reay, D. and Mirza, H. (2005) Doing parental involvement differently: black women's participation as educators and mothers in black supplementary schooling, in *Activating Participation: Parents and Teachers Working Together towards Partnership* (eds G. Crozier and D. Reay) Trentham Books, Stoke on Trent, pp. 137–154.

Roffey, S., Noble, T. and Stringer, P. (2008) Editorial. *Educational and Child Psychology*, **25** (2), 4–7.

Rogoff, B. (1991) The joint socialization of development by young children, in *Child Development in Social Context 2: Learning to Think* (eds P. Light, S. Sheldon and M. Woodhead), Routledge, London, pp. 67–96.

Rogoff, B. (2003) *The Cultural Nature of Human Development*, Oxford University Press, Oxford.

Roskos, K. and Chistie, J. (2001) Examining the play-literacy interface: a critical review and future directions. *Journal of Early Childhood Literacy*, **1** (1), 59–89.

Russell, K. and Granville, S. (2005) *Parents' Views on Improving Parental Involvement in Children's Education*, Scottish Executive, Edinburgh.

Saloviita, T., Italinna, M. and Leinonen, E. (2003) Explaining the parental stress of fathers and mothers caring for a child with intellectual disability: a double ABCX model. *Journal of Intellectual Disability Research*, **47** (4–5), 300–312.

Schmidt Neven, R. (2008) The promotion of emotional well-being for children, parents and families: what gets in the way? *Educational and Child Psychology*, **25** (2), 8–18.

Scott, W. (2001) Listening and learning, in *Experiencing Reggio Emilia: Implications for Pre-School Provision* (eds L. Abbott and C. Nutbrown), Open University Press, Maidenhead, pp. 21–29.

Scottish Executive (2007) *Reaching Out to Families*, Scottish Executive, Edinburgh.

Scottish Office (1998) *New Community Schools Prospectus*, www.scotland. gov.uk (accessed 3 March 2009).

Sheldon, B. and Voorhis, F. (2004) Partnership programs in U.S. schools: their development and relationship to family involvement outcomes. *School Effectiveness and School Improvement*, **15** (2), 125–148.

Swap, S. (1993) *Developing Home-School Partnerships: From Concepts to Practice*, Teachers College Press, New York.

Sylva, K., Melhuish, E., Sammons, P., Siraj-Blatchford, I, Taggart, B. and Elliot, K. (2004) *The Effective Provision of Pre-School Education Project (EPPE): Findings from the Pre-School Period*, Institute of Education, London.

Tett, L. (2005) Inter-agency partnerships and integrated community schools: a Scottish perspective. *Support for Learning*, **20** (4), 156–161.

Thomas, G. and Loxley, A. (2001*)* *Deconstructing Special Education and Constructing Inclusion*, 2nd edn, Open University Press, Milton Keynes.

Thornton, L. and Brunton, P. (2005) *Understanding the Reggio Approach*, David Fulton, London.

Tikly, L., Haynes, J. Caballero, C., Hill, J. and Gilborn, D. (2006) *Evaluation of Aiming High: African Caribbean Achievement Project*, Department for Education and Skills Publications, Nottingham.

Vincent, C. (1996) *Parents and Teachers: Power and Participation*, Falmer Press, London.

Vincent, C. (2001) Social class and parental agency. *Journal of Education Policy*, **16** (4), 347–364.

Wallander, J. and Varni, J. (1998) Effects of pediatric chronic physical disorder on child and family adjustment. *Journal of Child Psychology and Psychiatry*, **39** (1), 29–46.

Waller, W. (1932) *The Sociology of Teaching*, John Wiley & Sons, Inc, New York.

Webster, A., Feiler, A., Webster, V. and Lovell, C. (2004) Parental perspectives on early intensive intervention for children diagnosed with autistic spectrum disorder. *Journal of Early Childhood Research*, **2** (1), 25–49.

Welsh Assembly (2004) *Children and Young People: Rights to Action*, National Assembly for Wales, Cardiff.

Welshman, J. (2006a) *Underclass: A History of the Excluded 1880–2000*, Hambledon Continuum, London.

Welshman, J. (2006b) From the cycle of deprivation to social exclusion: five continuities. *The Political Quarterly*, **77** (4), 475–484.

Welshman, J. (in press) From Head Start to Sure Start: reflections on policy transfer. *Children and Society*.

Whalley, M. (2001) *Involving Parents in Their Children's Learning*, Sage, London.

Wilkin, A., Kinder, K., White R., Atkinson, M. and Doherty, P. (2003) *Towards the Development of Extended Schools*, Department for Education and Skills, London.

Williams, B., Williams, J. and Ullman, A. (2002) *Parental Involvement in Education*, Department for Education and Skills, London.

Williamson, D., Cullen, J. and Lepper, C. (2006) Checklists to narratives in special education. *Australian Journal of Early Childhood*, **31** (2), 20–29.

Wrigley, J. (2000) Foreword, in *Home Advantage: Social Class and Parental Intervention in Elementary Education* (ed. Lareau, A), Rowman and Littlefield, Lanham, pp. vii–xvi.

Zigler, E. (1989) Addressing the nation's child care crisis: the school of the twenty-first century. *American Journal of Orthopsychiatry*, **59**, 484–491.

Index

Engaging 'Hard to Reach' Parents: Teacher–Parent Collaboration to Promote Children's Learning By Anthony Feiler © 2010 John Wiley & Sons, Ltd